Praise

"Diverse Achievers is a gift to early education. It comes at such a vital time as we help our youngest to understand the value of individual differences while, at the same time, applauding our common humanity. Storytelling works especially when we are guided through it with questions that provoke thinking. Thanks to Irene and Gary for helping all of us seek truth."

— **David Magill**, EdD, Director Emeritus, University of Chicago Laboratory Schools

"Diverse Achievers is a powerful resource for teachers to make inclusion an ongoing part of instruction. The break down that shows books for both male and female achievers, self-esteem, history, and questions for discussion helps to simplify instruction and planning."

— **Tiffany Sudler**, Teacher, School District of Philadelphia

"What a delicious educational resource for parents, teachers and other human services professionals to use when starting conversations about the contributions of other racial/ethnic groups in shaping the American culture we live in today.

This compilation of children's books as tools for having tough conversations is simply ingenious. Why? Because of the way it's organized, the rich selection of topics/books and the fact that it is user friendly. This is a tall order for any author(s) to handle complex issues with a stimuli that directs ways for adults to discuss diverse achievers with young people. The contexts of 'Jim Crow', restrictive immigration laws and fear of losing power in the midst of rapid social change is unsettling for many Americans.

Teachers and parents will simply love the range of books connected to grade levels and the guided tours to help them ask meaningful questions. There is no dogma. Readers are free to help children explore values in the context of their personal experiences. There are questions on social problems children experience in schools and communities. This approach is value free and non-judgmental, so the teachers and parents can help loved ones define their own values.

I cannot say enough about this book. I highly recommend it for educators and families who are navigating the complexities of race, class, gender and physical/mental abilities. It prepares us to develop skills of racial literacy and is a great resource for diversity consultants."

— **Portia Hunt**, PhD, President, Eclipse Management Consultant Group and Executive Director, National Center for Family Recovery, Licensed Psychologist

Diverse
ACHIEVERS

A guide for parents and teachers
on using children's literature
to promote self-esteem and an
understanding that anyone
can become an achiever

Irene Eizen and Gary Plummer

Re think

First published in Great Britain in 2022 by
Rethink Press (www.rethinkpress.com)

To Philip and Tess Etkowicz, my mother and father, of blessed memory, who instilled in me the values that made this work possible. I wish I could share this work with you.

IE

To my youngest granddaughters, Malaya, 5, and Shayley, 7. Malaya wants to be a scientist and Shayley wants to be an artist. To my only grandson, Shah, who is not yet 1, but who will soon discover what he wants to be.

GP

Contents

Foreword

In the spirit of what makes education the noblest of professions, the authors of *Diverse Achievers* intrinsically understand how the power of learning is most effectively harnessed through an inclusive curriculum capable of chronicling the lived experiences of individuals who look like or come from similar backgrounds as the students we educate. Such a curriculum, guided by exceptional teachers who are committed to relentlessly adapting and interrogating their own practice, creates an opportunity for an ever-changing and increasingly diverse world to serve as a meaningful platform for student engagement and success.

Although they have retired after long and successful careers as K–12 educators, Irene Eizen and Gary Plummer remain steadfastly committed to the promotion of excellence and inclusion in teaching and learning. Despite their disciplinary expertise in mathematics, Eizen and

Plummer also appreciate the fundamental importance of literacy as the foundation of educational attainment and student success, regardless of zip code, race, gender, sexuality, disability and/or socio-economic status.

The title, *Diverse Achievers*, has been carefully constructed to avoid the debates that permeate public education these days, which often unproductively pit competing notions of opportunity and achievement against one another. The book's primary aim is to celebrate individuals and narratives that demonstrate overcoming adversity and different kinds of discrimination and racism. In doing so, Eizen and Plummer graciously share with students, parents and teachers, the language of possibility and hope at a time when our nation is so sadly divided and polarized.

The book serves as an open invitation to current and future teachers to employ works of literature that inspire self-esteem and achievement, while also promoting critical opportunities for students to analyze the historical and current day-to-day realities facing families and communities struggling to overcome inequities and injustices. The contributors thoughtfully construct brief lesson plans or guiding questions for teachers and parents to use when highlighting how literary works can enhance student engagement and learning. Eizen and Plummer's grounded method for promoting self-esteem and effective teaching and learning also serves as an enduring reminder of the significance of family and community in the successful education of children.

As Dr. Eizen so poignantly notes in the book's Introduction, as the daughter of immigrants and Holocaust survivors, she knows all too well the dampening impact of injustice and discrimination. Yet rather than succumb to the generational effects of an unfathomable tragedy and horrific loss, Irene refused to be denied the opportunity to achieve, and bolstered by the love and encouragement of others, she became the first member of her family to attend and graduate from college.

Irene's story, like the works of literature included in the book, continues to resonate with and inspire current and future students to achieve, particularly, albeit not exclusively, from diverse backgrounds. *Diverse Achievers* represents an important contribution to the field and is a testimony to teaching as a principled "calling" that speaks to both the heart and minds of educators and students alike.

Gregory Anderson, PhD, Dean and Professor of Higher Education, College of Education and Human Development, Temple University

Introduction

By Irene Eizen

Why did I write this book?

My parents were immigrants and Holocaust survivors. They did not speak of the terrible events they must have witnessed or the losses they endured, but instead they taught the lessons of the Holocaust and a love of freedom and equality. They made success in education and goal setting into imperatives for me. Many children do not have an influencer in their lives to help them set high standards to aim for, and more importantly to guide them over the bumps in the road of life.

I am the first person in my family to go to college, and as a result the first person with an advanced and terminal degree and the first person to become a teacher. My parents were diverse achievers in their own way, but just as no books will be written about them, no books will be written about most of the influencers and diverse achievers on whose shoulders they stood.

This book highlights the lives, challenges, and accomplishments of diverse achievers. Embedded in much of the children's literature I have chosen for this work are the ways in which each diverse achiever learned and applied with rigor the skills that made them great. In many texts there will be connections between diverse achievers and how people important in their lives helped them to achieve greatness, although it is impossible to predict which individuals will benefit from these contacts and influences.

One of my goals in this book is to emphasize the importance of perseverance and hard work as components of great achievement, by raising thoughtful questions around how the diverse achievers came to become accomplished and the challenges they faced, sometimes just because they looked different from the majority. It took many of the subjects of this work years to become diverse achievers. They could have given up, but instead they persisted.

Not everyone has the benefit of strong shoulders to stand on, especially when they are young. It is my hope that young readers will find self-confidence in knowing that, even though a mentor or role model might not immediately be part of their personal circle of influencers, they could, at some point in their lives, be there. I also hope readers can learn how to apply the same principles the mentors of the diverse achievers in this book used to benefit those achievers.

Suggestions for using this book

Children's literature is an outstanding medium through which children and adults can learn about diverse achievers, and much of what needs mending in our society today can be addressed with children in the school setting and in their homes as families read together. I have written this book to enhance this learning opportunity by stimulating discussion and critical thinking about lessons of fairness, tolerance, and real rather than perceived differences and stereotypes. This process can be teacher- and parent-centered, and the book is designed to be a guide for parents, children, and teachers to get the most out of the stories by building an awareness of some of the characteristics common to many achievers, and some of their challenges as well.

For African Americans, currently the largest racial minority in the United States, "the legacy of slavery continues to have an impact on black people's position in American society today" (Pew Research, page 8).

Many of the books in this first volume highlight the lives, challenges, and subsequent triumphs of slaves and/or their offspring.

Although this first volume will concentrate on diverse achievers who are primarily African-American, with books written largely by African-American authors, it is intended for an audience as varied as the population of America, the whole melting pot. An important goal of this book is for children and parents who are not African-American to enjoy reading about people who differ from them and most of the population in looks only, helping to break down stereotypes of bigotry and discrimination, and for families of African-American readers to learn from the stories about other African Americans who are outstanding contributors to our American society.

One common thread will be noted: each achiever took advantage of opportunity, and accomplished goals through hard work and perseverance, often in the face of adversity. This is highlighted in the discussion questions.

There are eighty-two works of children's literature referenced in the first volume, written largely by African-American authors and many illustrated by African-American illustrators. They address issues such as the impact of slavery, civil rights, equality and equity, education, ongoing discrimination, and racism. The work also considers other timely related topics and societal concerns.

For each of the eighty-two books there is a series of questions for discussion, written responses, activities, and/or research. There is also a suggested grade level range for the use of the book. In many cases, the books are best read by the parent/teacher to the child(ren). In some cases, the parent or teacher may decide the book can be read independently by students. The questions can be used in whichever ways the parent/teacher deems appropriate. Following the questions, for many of the books there are suggested books for further reading, again by the teacher to the class, by the parent to or with the child, or independently by the child. The choice is left to the teacher/parent.

Teachers at all grade levels should be able to find ways to address key subjects by harnessing the discussion questions individually with their students, in groups, or in an entire classroom discussion. Teachers may also become the catalyst for encouraging parents and children to read at home about the diverse heroes in these volumes. This can lead to discussions between students and their parents and other adult mentors, which teachers can revisit in their classrooms.

Readers will learn how racial, religious, and other forms of discrimination have made it difficult for diverse achievers of earlier generations and still today to reach their goals. They succeeded despite these headwinds. I hope that this will lead to a grass roots understanding that our society can no longer tolerate discrimination of any kind. Stamp it out once and for all. How wonderful it will be if we can arrive at a time when everyone has an equal chance to become a diverse achiever.

I have reviewed hundreds of children's books to arrive at the ones I have selected and the questions I have set out. This volume contains a selective bibliography of other contemporary children's literature that I intend to be helpful for readers as they expand their horizons with their families and as teachers seek more opportunities with their classes. The bibliography may also be a way for parents and adult mentors to develop discussion around literature not covered directly in this volume by applying similar questions to those I have outlined here. The bibliography alone may be a resource for families and educators to find more stories about diverse achievers.

Children need role models who look like they do. There are hundreds of diverse achievers from minority populations who are unknown to most people and who deserve recognition for their achievements, and whom others can emulate. Children also need role models who look different but have similar targets for achievement to break down barriers and to challenge implicit discrimination.

Reference

Pew Research. "Views on Race in America: Social and Demographic Trends." 2019. www.pewresearch.org

PART ONE
COURAGEOUS CONVERSATIONS

The Undefeated

by Kwame Alexander   Grades 4–8

Summary

A beautifully illustrated book of portraits of African Americans who withstood unspeakable trauma, over-came difficult obstacles of slavery and racism, and rose above these atrocious acts to succeed. Many famous African Americans from the past and the present are referred to in this story of bravery and success. A brief biography of each of these heroes is included at the back of the book.

Alexander, Kwiame. *The Undefeated.* New York: Houghton Mifflin Harcourt, 2019.

Questions for discussion, written responses, and/or research

1. The book celebrates those who were undefeated. Included in this are several categories named by the authors. Let's examine some of these categories and the person(s) included in each. Who were or are they and what did they contribute to the rise of African Americans through tremendously difficult circumstances?

- The unforgettable

- The undeniable

- The unafraid

- The righteous ones

- The unspeakables

- The unlimited dreamers and doers

- The unbelievables

2. Select one of the Undefeated, research their life and accomplishments, and why they should be included in the book. Be prepared to give a summary of each one to your class.

3. This book was awarded the Caldecott Medal and designated as a Newberry Honor book. Research these awards and discuss why you think *The Undefeated* received both of these awards.

Mixed Me!

by Taye Diggs   Grades K–3

Summary

Mixed Mike is just right. He is the perfect blend of parents from different races, one dark and one light. This uplifting book addresses a topic that has become increasingly important. Read about Mike and how he deals with being biracial, or of mixed race.

Diggs, Taye. *Mixed Me!* New York: Macmillan, 2015.

Questions for discussion, written responses, and/or research

1. Mixed Mike has parents of difference races, one dark and one light. Why does Mike not like that he is sometimes called Mixed-Up Mike?

2. Children whose parents are two different races are called biracial. Which part of the word biracial indicates that it refers to two?

3. When his friends tell Mike that "his mom and dad" (page 11) don't match, what is Mike's reaction?

4. Why does he say people look at him in a funny way? Why shouldn't this happen?

5. What do his parents say about his skin color not being the same as either one of theirs?

6. "There are so many flavors [of cereal in the illustration] to savor and taste. Why pick only one color or face?" What is Mike referring to and what is he saying?

7. What is Mike's feeling about basing his choice of friends on one race? What do you think about this?

8. Mike compares himself to a combo plate. What does he mean?

9. When people say something about his hair, what is Mike's reaction? Why?

10. What have you learned from the story?

Strange Fruit: Billie Holiday And The Power Of A Protest Song

by Gary Golio   Grades 6–8

Summary

A beautifully illustrated story about Billie Holiday's professional life as a singer. The title of the book is from a song with which Billie closed all of her shows from 1939 onward, "Strange Fruit." The song, written by Abel Meeropol, addressed the brutal practice of lynching, which was done by mobs of people, mostly to African Americans, as a form of punishment for a perceived misdeed. "Strange Fruit" turned out to be Billie's signature song of protest at how African Americans were treated in the United States during the late nineteenth century and well into the twentieth century.

Golio, Gary. *Strange Fruit: Billie Holiday and the Power of a Protest Song*. Minneapolis: Millbrook Press, 2017.

Questions for discussion, written responses, and/or research

1. Who was Artie Shaw? How was he responsible for Billie Holiday's early success as a singer?

2. What were some of the things Billie was told not to do while she performed at the Lincoln Hotel in New York City? Why wasn't she allowed to do these things?

3. Billie had a difficult childhood. What were some of her early traumatic experiences? Why did these experiences occur?

4. As difficult as life got for Billie, what always gave her hope?

5. Billie was part of the Harlem Renaissance. What was the Harlem Renaissance? Under which circumstances did it occur?

6. Which genres of music did Billie Holiday sing? Do they exist today?

7. Billie experienced racism and discrimination during her professional life. Name some of the things she had to do to hide her race. How was her light skin an impediment to her performing?

8. What made Harlem's Cotton Club so famous? Give examples of some of the negative things that also occurred at this famed club.

9. Who was Barney Josephson? What did he do to combat racism?

10. Who was Abel Meeropol? What did he do to protest against racism and how did he get Billie Holiday involved?

11. What were some of Billie's concerns about singing "Strange Fruit"?

12. How did Billie plan to deal with the audience reaction to this song?

13. What concerns did Billie's mother have about her singing this song?

14. Read and discuss the biography of Billie Holiday, which is found at the end of the book. What were some of the high and low points of her life?

A Kids Book About Diversity

by Charnaie Gordon   Grades 2–8

Summary

As the author suggests in the introduction to the book, "Consider how different the world would look if we all just accepted each other for who we are" (page i). Diversity is showcased and defined throughout the book using numerous real-world examples. This book acts as a catalyst for grown-ups and kids to have an important conversation about diversity, and helps to answer questions about how people can be sensitive to the term and concept.

Gordon, Charnaie. *A Kids Book About Diversity.* Portland, OR: A Kids Book About, Inc., 2021.

Note to teachers/parents: The meaning of cisgender is defined in a footnote at the bottom of the page on which the word appears. Please use your discretion to define this word as appropriate with different grade levels.

Questions for discussion, written responses, and/or research

1. Before reading and discussing the book, think about what the word "diversity" means to you. Record your response to refer back to once you have finished reading.

2. Use the first four pages of the book to answer the questions it poses. Your response will help formulate an understanding of the meaning of diversity.

3. How does the author define diversity?

4. Give some examples of characteristics that make people diverse.

5. How does diversity make each person unique?

6. The author states that, "Being different is what makes us special" (page 14). What does the author mean by this statement?

7. Why does the author feel it is important to have a superhero who looks like you?

8. The author lists thirteen differences we see in a diverse world, starting with the word "people" and ending with the word "holidays." What other differences do we see in a diverse world? Use your answers to extend the list.

9. What does the phrase "we should embrace diversity" (page 25) mean to you?

10. What does the term "kids of color" mean? Why is it critical that kids of color have role models who look like them?

11. According to the book, knowing and seeing role models of color can lead to good things. What are they?

12. How does seeing people like you build your self-esteem and theirs?

13. Why did the author, as a child, understand the true meaning of diversity? How did this make her feel?

14. What changed her diminished attitude about her self-worth?

15. Who is Oprah Winfrey? Google her to find out. What good things happened to the author as a child as a result of seeing someone she could relate to?

16. How has progress been made with respect to diversity in today's society? What still needs to be done to continue the progress?

17. The author speaks about diversity with respect to people in wheelchairs or people with disabilities. Do you know any people with disabilities? Without using names, how are they disabled?

18. Look up the term "indigenous." Who does this term refer to? Do you know any indigenous people?

19. Name some of the ways in which your neighborhood is diverse.

20. The author asks us to think about how we can have more diversity in our lives. What can each of us do to accomplish this individually?

A Kids Book About Racism

by Jelani Memory   **Grades 3–8**

Summary

What is racism? Have you ever been a victim of racism? Adults and children should read this book to learn about this important topic.

Memory, Jelani. *A Kids Book About Racism.* Portland, OR: A Kids Book About, Inc., 2019.

Questions for discussion, written responses, and/or research

1. Jelani says he is of "mixed race." What does this term mean?

2. Jelani uses four terms to describe his race. What are they? We hear these terms in everyday conversations, on talk shows and in the news. Which ones are you familiar with?

3. We should all be proud of who we are and always respect those who don't look like us. Name some of your friends who are different from you and why you like and respect them. How are they different?

4. All people are different. We call that diversity. Diversity is an important human quality that we should respect. Why is diversity so important?

5. What do you think racism means? Have you heard this term used? In which context are you familiar with the term? Does racism apply only to skin color? Why?

6. List some characteristics of racism. Have you experienced it? If so, how?

7. Research the civil rights movement. In pairs, google four or five things about civil rights and discuss them with the class. Don't forget to cite your sources of information.

A Kids Book About Disabilities

by Kristine Napper   **Grades 3–8**

Summary

We all know or have seen a disabled person. The purpose of this book is to teach us how to talk about disabilities and how to behave and interact appropriately with disabled people. The author describes her own disability in the book, and suggests a number of ways we can make disabled people feel included.

Napper, Kristine. *A Kids Book About Disabilities.* Portland, OR: A Kids Book About, Inc., 2020.

Questions for discussion, written responses, and/or research

1. What is Spinal Muscular Atrophy (SMA)? What effect does it have on the body?

2. How has SMA affected Kristine?

3. How do some people react when they see Kristine?

4. Why do you think people react in this way?

5. What does Kristine think about having a disability? How does she see herself?

6. Name some of the things Kristine shares about her disability.

7. How does Kristine define "normal"?

8. What does Kristine say about kids' reactions to a person with a disability? What about adults' reactions?

9. While a disabled person can do many things on their own, what are some things Kristine may need help with?

10. Kristine uses the term "forced help." What does she mean by this term? When should someone help a disabled person, according to Kristine?

11. Kristine says it is OK to ask her nice questions. What are some questions you feel are appropriate to ask? What should you avoid asking her?

12. In what ways does the world need to change to help disabled people adjust to their disability?

13. There are several different types of disabilities. Name one and research its characteristics.

14. What can we do to support people with disabilities?

I Am Whole

by Shola Oz   Grades K–3

Summary

This is a work of fiction about an important topic. Biracial children are often made to feel uncomfortable in school and social settings. The young girl telling the story has a black mother and a white father. Rather than identify as black or white, she identifies as whole, the perfect mix of Mom and Dad. Her family is mixed and she loves everyone in it. She is proud of herself and her family and she feels lucky that she doesn't have to choose. An uplifting book for everyone.

Oz, Shola. *I Am Whole*. London: I Am Whole Books, 2020.

Questions for discussion, written responses, and/or research

1. The little girl who is telling the story is biracial. How does the prefix bi- help you understand the meaning of the word "biracial"?

2. Her extended family has members of each race, white and black, and she loves all of them. How does the illustration on pages 3 and 4 show the love of this family?

3. She is proud to be different. Her difference is that she is biracial. People have many differences which distinguish them from one another. What are some differences we can see? What are some differences we don't always see but know exist? How can we tell they exist?

4. Why should differences among people be celebrated?

5. As you listen to the story, pick out pairs of rhyming words and write them down or ask someone to write them down for you.

6. What is jollof? Use Google to find out. Have you ever eaten jollof? What does it taste like?

7. What do you think the girl means when she says her culture "is mixed in all the best ways" (page 13)?

8. What does it mean to "dress up in native to celebrate special days" (page 14)? Do you or your family dress up on special days? What are those days?

9. What did you learn from the story?

Select related children's literature

Diggs, Taye. *Mixed Me!* New York: Macmillan, 2015.

A Kids Book About Systemic Racism

by Jordan Thierry   Grades 3–8

Summary

Reminding us that, "We're living in a moment where racial injustice, implicit bias and inequality continue to thrive," (page 1) this book offers reasons for the continued existence of systemic racism.

Thierry, Jordan. *A Kids Book About Systemic Racism.* Portland, OR: A Kids Book About, Inc., 2020.

Questions for discussion, written responses, and/or research

1. "Systemic racism seems normal" (pages 12–13). What does the author mean by this statement?

2. What is the author's main purpose in writing this book?

3. What does racism look like?

4. What is the difference between racism and systemic racism?

5. List ways in which the author experienced systemic racism as a child and as a teenager.

6. Systemic racism is a pattern. What does this mean?

7. How did systemic racism begin? Summarize how it evolved and why.

8. What is the Black Lives Matter movement? Where, when, and why has it been in the recent news?

9. How does systemic racism affect people's lives today?

10. The term "equal access" is critical to ending systemic racism. What does equal access entail?

11. How can we work together to end systemic racism?

12. Jordan Thierry is black and states that when he was a child, he rarely read a book by a black author. Why was this? Research some famous black authors and what each one wrote.

A Kids Book About Bullying

by Elizabeth Tom   **Grades 3–8**

Summary

The author writes about her experiences of being bullied and offers suggestions for ways other people can put an end to bullying.

Tom, Elizabeth. *A Kids Book About Bullying.* Portland, OR: A Kids Book About, Inc., 2020.

Questions for discussion, written responses, and/or research

1. Name some of the ways Elizabeth's disability, cerebral palsy, is evident to other people.

2. What is the main topic of Elizabeth's book? Why did she decide to write this book?

3. List some of the ways one person can bully another.

4. What is Elizabeth's definition of bullying? Do you agree with it? Give reasons for your answer.

5. Elizabeth says that sometimes she was bullied by "being taunted and called names" (page 20). What does "taunt" mean?

6. Do you think Elizabeth should have told her parents about the bullying? What could they have done to help? How should her school have reacted?

7. In fifth grade Elizabeth showed her friend a note she had received from another kid containing hurtful statements about her. Elizabeth's friend showed the note to the teacher. How do you think the teacher should have responded?

8. Do you think showing the note to the teacher was sensible? Why?

9. Do you think it was a good idea to also let her parents know about the note? Explain your answer.

10. What emotions did Elizabeth have as a result of being bullied?

11. Have you ever been bullied? Describe how you felt.

12. Elizabeth explains that she began bullying other kids as a result of being bullied. Do you think this was a good idea or a bad idea?

13. What does Elizabeth suggest you do if you know someone who is being bullied? Why do you think this is good advice?

Separate Is Never Equal

by Duncan Tonatiuh   Grades 4–8

Summary

The Mendez family moved from Santa Ana, California to Westminster, California, a small town with a neighborhood school. When their aunt took the three Mendez children and their cousins to enroll at the local school, the Mendez children were not allowed to enroll and were told to go to the Mexican school instead. Born in America and speaking perfect English, Sylvia Mendez could not understand why, along with her siblings, she couldn't go to the local school. She figured out it was because of her brown skin and thick curly hair. The Mendez family decided to start a lawsuit, and the result helped end segregation in California. Theirs was a fight for justice and equality.

Tonatiuh, Duncan. *Separate Is Never Equal.* New York: Abrams, 2014.

Questions for discussion, written responses, and/or research

1. This true story happened between 1944 and 1947 and the result of the lawsuit set the stage for the

Supreme Court case Brown vs. Board of Education in 1954. Research Brown vs. Board of Education. What was this case about? What was the outcome?

2. There are numerous Spanish phrases throughout the book, some of which are translated into English. Others can be translated based on the context. As you encounter these phrases, determine what they mean.

3. What were some of the differences between the all-white neighborhood school and the Mexican school?

4. List some of the reasons given to the Mendez family for not being able to enroll their children in the neighborhood school and for having to send them to the Mexican school instead.

5. In response to the Mendez children being denied the right to attend the neighborhood school, Mr. Mendez organized a group of parents of Mexican-American children. How did the parents feel about signing the petition asking for equal opportunity for these children? Why did they feel this way?

6. What were some of the other discriminatory practices Mexican Americans encountered? What did Mr. Mendez and his lawyer Mr. Marcus do in response?

7. How many children in Orange County, California were affected by this unfair rule of going to the Mexican school?

8. When the lawsuit was filed and the trial started, what reason did the superintendent of one of the districts give for the students being made to go to the Mexican school? Why was this a poor reason?

9. What other things did Mr. Kent, the superintendent, have to say about Mexican-American children having to attend the Mexican school?

10. What did the education specialists called to the stand during the trial say about the segregation of children?

11. What was the outcome of the trial? How long did it take the judge to render his decision?

12. The school board appealed the decision. What does this mean?

13. What civil rights organizations supported the court's decision?

14. The outcome became a law. What did the law say?

15. When Sylvia finally went to the neighborhood school, how was she greeted by many of the other students?

PART TWO
CELEBRATING DIFFERENCES

Hair Love

by Matthew Cherry   **Grades K–3**

Summary

Zuri has amazing hair. Her hair tends to do what it wants and it takes the skill of a loving father to create styles for Zuri. Today is a special day and Zuri needs a special style. Dad is like a professional hairstylist with Zuri's hair and creates one that is perfect for her.

Cherry, Matthew A. *Hair Love*. New York: Penguin Random House, 2019.

Questions for discussion, written responses, and/or research

1. Dad had a nickname for Zuri. What was it? Do you have a nickname? How did you get it?

2. Why do you think the author titled the book, *Hair Love*?

3. While Dad was working on Zuri's hairstyle, what was Mom doing? How do you know?

4. Dad tried many different hairstyles that Zuri didn't like. What did Dad do next? What did he use to help him?

5. What were some of the things Dad did to come up with the perfect hairstyle for Zuri?

6. Was Dad used to styling Zuri's hair? What in the story helps you find your answer to this question?

7. When you want or need a special hairstyle, who creates it for you?

Select related children's literature

Barnes, Derrick and James, Gordon C. *Crown: An Ode to the Fresh Cut*. Chicago: Bolden, 2017.

Swain-Bates, Crystal. *Big Hair, Don't Care*. Walnut, CA: Goldest Karat Publishing, 2013.

Tarpley, Natasha Anastasia. *I Love My Hair*. New York: Little, Brown and Company Books for Young Readers, 1998.

Superheroes Are Everywhere

by Kamala Harris   **Grades K–5**

Summary

What is a superhero? Kamala Harris's book describes different types of superheroes and asks the reader to name some superheroes of their own. An uplifting and important book.

Harris, Kamala. *Superheroes Are Everywhere*. New York: Philomel Books, 2019.

Questions for discussion, written responses, and/or research

1. According to Kamala Harris, what is a superhero?

2. What important lesson did Kamala's mother teach her? How did this lesson make her mom a superhero?

3. Who are the superheroes in your life? Why do you consider each a superhero?

4. In what ways can each of us be a superhero?

5. Kamala's mother would make her and her sister, Maya, an "unbirthday party" when they were sad. What do you think an unbirthday party is?

6. Kamala's grandmother "used her smarts and her voice to speak out for women who were being emotionally hurt and to teach them to be healthy" (page 9). How could women in today's society get hurt by not having the opportunities men have?

7. What can we do to stay emotionally healthy?

8. How does Kamala address bullying in the story? How did she confront one of her best friend's bullies?

9. Kamala says that teachers are superheroes. In what ways can a teacher be a superhero?

10. A neighbor can also be a superhero. How was Kamala and Maya's neighbor a superhero?

11. "Heroes" work hard. Who are some people you know who work hard? What type of work do they do? What type of work do you think you will do and how will you work hard?

12. Kamala Harris became a lawyer. She was inspired by some brilliant lawyers, including Thurgood Marshall, Constance Baker Motley, and Charles Hamilton Houston. How did each of these lawyers contribute to the protection of all the people in the United States? You could research this in small groups with other students.

13. Who is Kamala Harris? What important job has she had since January 20, 2021?

14. What is the hero's code? Stand up and take the code with your teacher.

15. Inside the front and back covers of the book are numerous photos of Kamala and her family. There is also a timeline of important events in Kamala's life near the end of the book. Be sure to look at and discuss all of this useful information.

Activity: Collect pictures of you, your family, and other important people in your life. Mount each picture on paper with a brief caption describing who or what the picture shows and do this in chronological order. Start from the date you were born and end close to the current date. If you can't find a picture for a special date on your timeline, draw one.

Select related children's literature

Clinton, Chelsea. *She Persisted: 13 American Women Who Changed the World.* New York: Philomel Books, 2017.

Most Days

by Michael Leannah   **Grades K–4**

Summary

It may seem that most days are routine days when nothing out of the ordinary happens, but with each new day come extraordinary events and things. What are some of these extraordinary things? What changes do we notice each day? The children in the story discover that many new things happen on just an ordinary day.

Leannah, Michael. *Most Days*. Thomaston, ME: Tilbury House, 2021.

Questions for discussion, written responses, and/or research

1. What are some new things you noticed today that are different from yesterday?

2. What are some routine things you do each day? Do your routines ever change? Why? Give some examples.

3. In the story, it says that things may not happen in the same way on two different days. Can you find some examples?

4. What are some of the differences we would notice between a winter and summer day? Which season is your favorite and why?

5. According to the story, what are "some good things [that can happen] in the ordinary minutes of an ordinary day" (page 21)? Use the illustrations to help you answer this question.

6. How can an ordinary day become extraordinary?

Select related children's literature

Leannah, Michael. *Most People.* Thomaston, ME: Tilbury House, 2017.

Most People

by Michael Leannah   **Grades K–4**

Summary

Most people are good people. Very few are bad, and even the bad people have good in them. This book promotes the diversity and goodness in people and has lovely words and illustrations to support its premise and lead to a productive discussion.

Leannah, Michael. *Most People.* Thomaston, ME: Tilbury House, 2017.

Questions for discussion, written responses, and/or research

1. List some of the things that most people love to do. Which of these do you love to do?

2. What are some of the things that good people are doing in the story? Use the illustrations to help answer this question.

3. There are a few people who act badly. What might they do?

4. The author compares lining up all the good people in one line to putting all the bad people in one room. Which of the two will have the greater number of people? How do you know from the story?

5. "People who do bad things can change" (page 14). What is the young man in the illustration doing that shows this?

6. What good things can a community do? Have you ever been involved in a community event in which people were doing good things? What was the event and what were people doing?

7. All different kinds of people are shown in the illustrations. Can you tell if someone is a good person or not by the way they look? Explain your answer.

Select related children's literature

Leannah, Michael. *Most Days.* Thomaston, ME: Tilbury House, 2021.

Share Your Rainbow

by R.J. Palacio   **Grades 2–5**

Summary

With an introduction by R.J. Palacio, this book is a compilation of artwork depicting different rainbows in various life contexts and suggests seeing the world through its beautiful, colorful depictions.

Palacio, R.J. *Share Your Rainbow.* New York: Penguin Random House, 2020.

Questions for discussion, written responses, and/or research.

1. Discuss each painting and how it relates to the printed words. How does each page depict a rainbow in life?

I Can Write The World

by Joshunda Sanders   Grades 4–8

Summary

Ava Murray is an eight-year-old girl who lives in the Bronx. She wants to be a journalist. She describes the sights and sounds of her neighborhood as the confluence of many nationalities, with the people using their creativity to paint and make music from their countries. The Bronx is so much more than what the nightly newscasters say it is through their reporting of bad things. Ava knows all the good things that happen in her neighborhood and wants to be a journalist who reports on them. Colorful and beautiful illustrations support the story.

Sanders, Joshunda. *I Can Write the World*. Houston: Six Foot Press, 2019.

Questions for discussion, written responses, and/or research

1. Do you think Ava is really Joshunda Sanders, this book's author and a journalist, and that this is a story about her childhood? Give reasons for your answer.

2. What is graffiti? Why did a girl get arrested for painting graffiti on plain outside walls?

3. This girl painted beautiful pictures, but broke the rules, according to Ava's mother. What should she have done before she painted the walls?

4. When you watch the evening news, are most of the stories about bad things happening or good things happening? What gives you this impression?

5. What did Ava's mom say about creativity? What types of creative things have you done?

6. What did Ava's mom tell Ava about how she and her friends learned music and art as kids when these courses were not available to them as students?

7. How did Ava's mom compare a nightly news report on TV to a window frame?

8. How did this influence the type of journalism Ava wanted to report?

9. Why is the book entitled *I Can Write the World*?

The Day You Begin

by Jacqueline Woodson   Grades K–4

Summary

Each of us is different and our differences are to be celebrated. Unfortunately, sometimes they are not and sometimes they are even ridiculed. This is an uplifting story about a young girl who feels like an outsider until she uses her voice to share her stories. Then she finds out how alike she is to the other children and how her differences are what make her special.

Woodson, Jacqueline. *The Day You Begin*. New York: Nancy Paulson, 2018.

Questions for discussion, written responses, and/or research

1. According to the story, how are people different from each other? Name some differences not mentioned in the story.

2. Differences should be celebrated. What does this mean?

3. What was the class's reaction when Rigoberto introduced himself? How did the teacher help the class think differently about Rigoberto?

4. What were some of the things the students did during summer vacation? Why did the girl narrating the story feel like an outsider?

5. How did her perception of her summer vacation change once she opened up to the class about her stories?

6. Select some different pages in the book and describe how the illustrations support the storyline.

7. How was staying home in the summer like going everywhere for the girl and her sister?

8. What happens on the day you begin?

Select related children's literature

Carroll, Kevin. *A Kids Book About Belonging.* Portland, OR: A Kids Book About, Inc., 2019.

Murphy, Frank. *A Boy Like You.* Ann Arbor, MI: Sleeping Bear Press, 2019.

Murphy, Frank and Murphy, Carla. *A Girl Like You.* Ann Arbor, MI: Sleeping Bear Press, 2020.

PART THREE
DIVERSE FEMALE ACHIEVERS

Lizzie Demands A Seat!

by Beth Anderson   Grades 2–6

Summary

Before Rosa Parks, there was Elizabeth Jennings, who was refused a seat on a streetcar because she was African-American. Told by the conductor to wait for the next car, which is for "your people," her reaction was admirable. Facing sometimes insurmountable racism, she actively pursued equality for African Americans. She demanded her rights in public and in the courts.

Anderson, Beth. *Lizzie Demands a Seat!* New York: Calkins Creek, 2020.

Questions for discussion, written responses, and/or research

1. Where did this story take place?

2. Briefly describe the episode, how Lizzie fought back, and the outcome of her riding on that streetcar. Where was Lizzie going? Why?

3. Why was the conductor so angry with Lizzie? Was it customary for a conductor to deny a seat to an

African-American person on a streetcar in New York City?

4. Why did Lizzie decide to take her case to court? What support did her church community give her?

5. Her lawyer was Chester Arthur. Research him to find out who he was.

6. What was Lizzie's profession? How did her focus on equality for all help her in her work?

7. What was the jury's verdict? How did the community and the streetcar company respond?

8. What did you learn from reading this story?

9. The streetcar incident happened in 1854 in New York City. How long before the Rosa Parks incident did this occur? You will have to do some research to find out.

Select related children's literature

Kudlinski, Kathleen. *Rosa Parks*. New York: Aladdin, 2001.

Madam C.J. Walker's Road To Success

by Donnette Black   Grades 5–8

Summary

Sarah Breedlove, a social activist who took the name of her third husband, C.J. Walker, was the first African-American self-made female millionaire in the United States. She was also a philanthropist, a civil rights and social activist, and an entrepreneur, having invented a line of hair products as a result of her own scalp ailment. Finding out that the hair products worked on other black women, she began to market her products, train other women to sell her products, and build a following so large she became a millionaire. She did many philanthropic things with her money. Read the story to learn about her life, her struggles, and triumphs.

Black, Donnette. *Madam C.J. Walker's Road to Success.* Bloomington: AuthorHouse, 2010.

Questions for discussion, written responses, and/or research

1. Sarah Breedlove had a difficult start in life. She married at fourteen and had her only child. What were some of the difficulties Sarah faced during her young years?

2. Sarah's first husband died when Sarah was twenty. What types of work did she have to do to make a living?

3. Education was important to Sarah. What did she save her money to do to help her daughter, A'Lelia? Was she successful?

4. Research Booker T. Washington to find out who he was.

5. After hearing Mrs. Washington speak at a state fair, Sarah made some decisions about her own life. What were some of these decisions?

6. How did Sarah get started in the hair product business?

7. Why did Sarah move to Denver? How did this help her haircare business?

8. Sarah believed that hard work, faith, and determination would get you closer to your goals (page 7). How would you apply this statement to your life?

9. Sarah used her self-created hair products to fix her hair, which was falling out. When a product worked on her hair, what did she decide to do to make sure it would be effective for everyone?

10. Sarah started her own business, keeping in contact with a man she had met in St. Louis named Charles Joseph Walker. They married in 1906. Why did Sarah change her name to Madam C.J. Walker?

11. What was Madam C.J. Walker's "Wonderful Hair Grower"? What did she do to market the product so that it would sell? Where did she first start selling her product?

12. Why did Madam C.J. Walker get other women involved in her business? What was she hoping to accomplish?

13. Madam C.J. Walker started selling other types of products. What were some of these products? How did she advertise them?

14. What does the expression "household name" mean?

15. What name do we give to the people Madam C.J. Walker referred to as "culturalists"?

16. Madam C.J. Walker faced racism. What happened at the movie theater? What did she do as a result of her experience of racism?

17. Why did she move her business to Indianapolis in 1910?

18. Once Madam C.J. Walker became rich and famous she began to do many philanthropic things with her money. What is philanthropy? What kinds of things did she do?

19. What is the NAACP? You may have to do some research to find out.

20. Madam C.J. Walker's products earned international acclaim. Which countries did she travel to to promote her products?

21. In 1918, she built a beautiful mansion in New York. Describe the mansion. Does it still exist?

22. Do Madam C.J. Walker's products still exist? Do some research to find out.

Fancy Party Gowns

by Deborah Blumenthal   Grades 2–6

Summary

By integrating quotes such as, "Ann thought about what she could do, not what she couldn't change" (page 6) into the text, this story promotes an attitude of acceptance and resourcefulness. Ann Lowe learned from her mother to be a fashion designer at the age of sixteen. Ann was African-American and as she became famous for her one-of-a-kind designs she faced many obstacles due to racism. The story is beautifully illustrated and uplifting, and explains why Ann persisted to become a famous fashion designer.

Blumenthal, Deborah. *Fancy Party Gowns*. New York: Little Bee Books, 2017.

Questions for discussion, written responses, and/or research

1. When Ann was a small child, she began to sew. How was she inspired?

2. Ann's great-grandmother had been a slave. Even though Ann was born free, what were some of the obstacles she faced due to racism as she was growing up?

3. What were the circumstances that caused Ann to take over her mother's sewing business? How old was Ann when she did this?

4. The words, "Ann thought about what she could do, not what she couldn't change" are written throughout the book. What were some situations Ann faced when she had to figure out what to do because she couldn't change the circumstances?

5. Which obstacle did Ann encounter when she went to design school in New York?

6. Ann received a special order for a wedding dress for Jacqueline Bouvier. Who was she and whom did she marry?

7. What did Ann do when she found ten of the sixteen dresses she had made for this wedding were ruined by a flood? Name some of the ways in which she focused, once again, on what she could do, not on what she couldn't change.

8. How did Ann deal with the butler in Newport when she tried to deliver all the dresses? What were the circumstances?

9. Ann Cole Lowe (her married name) still didn't become famous for all the beautiful dresses she designed and made for the wedding. Why was this?

10. What was the real reason Ann made such beautiful clothes?

WOKE

by Mahogany Browne   **Grades 3–8**

Summary

A brilliant anthology of poems written by women about issues of social justice, including discrimination, acceptance, using one's voice to speak out, racism, and compassion. The illustrations beautifully support each poem's message. Written for children aged 8–12, the poems seek to inspire readers to be activists for social justice through "softhandedness" (from the foreword).

Browne, Mahogany L. et al. *WOKE*. New York: Roaring Book Press, 2020.

Questions for discussion, written responses, and/or research

1. Choose one of the poems to read aloud. Stop at different points to discuss the meaning of the poem and what it is inspiring us to do.

2. Write your own poem as the authors suggest about an issue in social justice in which you are woke. Discuss how the illustrations of a poem add meaning.

3. What does the word "woke" mean to you?

Dancing Hands

by Margarita Engle   Grades 2–6

Summary

Theresa, who lived in Venezuela, learned to play the piano at a young age. Practicing to become skilled, she loved the beautiful sounds made by the music. A war in Venezuela caused Theresa and her family to move to New York, which was unfamiliar to them. There was also a war in the United States called the Civil War, but Theresa found that wherever there was music, people would come together. She became famous and played in many theaters with big orchestras. Her most amazing experience was being invited to play for President Abraham Lincoln.

Engle, Margarita. *Dancing Hands.* New York: Atheneum Books for Young Readers, 2019.

Questions for discussion, written responses, and/or research

1. How did Theresa learn to play the piano?

2. Throughout the book, music is compared to many of nature's sounds. Name some of these.

3. Music brought cheer when Theresa was sad. How did her many audiences of children and their parents react when Theresa played the piano?

4. Do you play any instruments? Have you ever performed before an audience? How do you feel when performing for others?

5. During which difficult time was Theresa asked to play the piano for President Lincoln? What did Theresa hope to accomplish by playing for the president?

6. How did Theresa's playing make the president feel?

7. At the end of the book there is an historical note about Theresa. Use this and your reading of the book to summarize her life in your own words.

Kamala Harris: Rooted In Justice

by Nikki Grimes   Grades 3–8

Summary

This book is the story of Vice President Kamala Harris's life before she was asked by the presidential candidate, Joseph Biden, to be his vice president in the 2020 United States election. A beautifully written and illustrated work of nonfiction, the reader will learn a great deal about Kamala, her hopes and dreams, her numerous achievements, her civil rights activism, and much more.

Grimes, Nikki. *Kamala Harris: Rooted in Justice.* New York: Atheneum Books for Young Readers, 2020.

Questions for discussion, written responses, and/or research

1. Kamala's name means lotus flower. The author states that Kamala's roots, unlike a lotus flower's roots, are deep. What are some of the examples from the story that illustrate how deep Kamala's roots in life are?

2. From an early age, Kamala was exposed to civil rights activism. What were some of the ways her parents involved her in early learning activities about civil rights?

3. Kamala Harris, current vice president of the United States, is the first African-American South Asian woman vice president of the United States. Where were her parents from? What were their professions?

4. When Kamala and her sister, Maya, were young, their parents divorced. Their mother took the girls to live in the flatlands of California. There Kamala was bussed to a school that was diverse in student population. What does this mean?

5. Which types of after-school activities did Kamala do? Name some of the famous writers and entertainers Kamala and Maya met during their Thursday night visits to the cultural center known as the Rainbow Room.

6. Shyamala, Maya and Kamala's mother, moved the family to Montreal during Kamala's first year of middle school. How did Kamala feel about this?

7. Which language did Kamala and Maya have to learn to live in Montreal?

8. Kamala and Maya showed their activism by supporting children playing outdoor sports on the front lawn of their apartment building. Why was this necessary and what was the result of their picketing?

9. Name some of the activities Kamala chose to do while a student at Howard, beyond her studies.

10. What is the exam that graduating law students must take to practice law? When did Kamala pass this test?

11. Which positions did Kamala hold as she journeyed through her career? Briefly describe each one and its location.

12. Before being selected as the running mate for presidential candidate Joseph Biden, what did Kamala announce on Martin Luther King's birthday in 2019?

13. Which characteristics helped to make Kamala successful as she climbed the ladder to the vice presidency?

14. Kamala went to Howard University. Google this university to find out more about it. Where is it located? Name some famous black Americans who went there.

15. In the story, the author states that Kamala's heroes included Thurgood Marshall, Constance Baker Motley, and Charles Hamilton Houston. Google these people and find out why Kamala considered them heroes.

Select related children's literature

Harris, Kamala. *Superheroes Are Everywhere*. New York: Philomel Books, 2019.

Harris, Meena. *Kamala and Maya's Big Idea*. New York: HarperCollins, 2020.

Sweet Dreams, Sarah

by Vivian Kirkfield   Grades 1–6

Summary

Sarah E. Jacobs, freed from slavery after the Civil War, was born into a family of seven children. Sarah's father was a carpenter and Sarah wanted to follow in his footsteps by learning carpentry skills and becoming an inventor, making things people would find practical. When the Great Migration occurred, in which freed slaves traveled to the North to get away from the ongoing racism and discrimination of the South, Sarah moved to Chicago, married Archibald Goode and started a family. She made beautiful and useful furniture, listened to her customers' needs, and came up with an invention, for which she applied for a patent. Read the story to find out about what she invented and her process of securing a U.S. patent.

Kirkfield, Vivian. *Sweet Dreams, Sarah.* Berkeley, CA: Creston Books, 2019.

Questions for discussion, written responses, and/or research

1. Read the story to find out what a patent is. Discuss with the class.

2. How did Sarah and her husband make a living?

3. What were the needs of Sarah's customers regarding furniture?

4. Sarah was full of hopes and dreams, and she listened to her customers. Which invention arose from this?

5. Sarah was a problem solver. How did her problem-solving skills lead to her invention?

6. Name some of the obstacles Sarah encountered in trying to complete her invention. How did she deal with them?

7. Why did Sarah need to get a patent? What happened with her application for a patent? What did she do as a result?

8. Use examples from the story to illustrate how Sarah was persistent.

9. The closing sentence of the book states, "She [Sarah] had built a life far away from slavery, where her sweet dreams could come through" (page 28). Recap the story to illustrate the truth of this statement.

10. At the back of the book is a timeline of black women patent holders. How many of their inventions have you heard of? Select one of the patent holders, research her and her invention, and write a short summary of what you find.

Select related children's literature

Black, Donnette. *Madam C.J. Walker's Road to Success.* Bloomington: AuthorHouse, 2010.

A Ride To Remember

by Sharon Langley
and Amy Nathan   Grades 3–8

Summary

Before the early 1960s, amusement parks in the United States were segregated and only allowed white people. Discrimination was rampant and in 1963, on Independence Day, African Americans who sought to end discrimination began peaceful protests. The protests continued until African Americans achieved equality. Sharon Langley, the author of this book, and her parents were the first African-American family to enter the newly desegregated Gwynn Oak Amusement Park in Baltimore, Maryland.

Langley, Sharon and Nathan, Amy. *A Ride to Remember.* New York: Abrams, 2020.

Questions for discussion, written responses, and/or research

1. How does the author, Sharon Langley, explain that everyone is equal on a carousel?

2. Sharon asked her parents why they couldn't go to the Grand Oaks Amusement Park in the late 1950s and early 1960s. What did they tell her?

3. How did Sharon's mother define segregation to her?

4. How did segregation conflict with the Golden Rule?

5. What kinds of things were black and white people not allowed to do together, according to Sharon's father?

6. Even though the amusement park rejected integration, some unfair laws in Baltimore had changed. What could black and white people now do together?

7. What actions did the townspeople take to desegregate the amusement park? On which day did they decide to do this? Why do you think this day was chosen? Were they successful?

8. Who were Lydia Phinney and Mabel Grant? What did they accomplish? How did the reporter who interviewed them help with the desegregation of the amusement park?

9. On August 28, 1963, Sharon's family went to the Gwynn Oak Amusement Park as the first African-American family to enter. What caused the park's owners to finally allow the park to be desegregated?

10. Who was Dr. Martin Luther King? Why was August 28, 1963 an important day to him?

11. Gwynn Oak Amusement Park eventually closed due to the destruction caused by a big storm. Most of the rides were destroyed except for the carousel. What happened to the carousel?

Select related children's literature

Allen, Tessa. *Sometimes People March.* New York: Balzer and Bray, 2020.

The Astronaut With A Song For The Stars: The Story Of Dr. Ellen Ochoa

by Julia Finley Mosca   Grades K–5

Summary

Ellen Ochoa is the grandchild of Mexican immigrants. Although born in the United States, she is of Latin origin. Her relatives dealt with racism in many forms. The story is about Ellen, her dreams, struggles, and, ultimately, her accomplishments.

Mosca, Julia Finley. *The Astronaut with a Song for the Stars: The Story of Dr. Ellen Ochoa.* Seattle: The Innovation Press, 2019.

Questions for discussion, written responses, and/or research

1. Ellen's first dream was to become a flutist. What advice did her mother give her to succeed? To become successful at something, what are some things we should do?

2. When Ellen started college, her interests changed. What did she now want to do?

3. What obstacles did she have to deal with to realize her dream at this point in her life? How was she motivated to overcome these obstacles? Who was her role model?

4. Ellen was innovative in pursuing her goal of becoming an astronaut. What did she accomplish before being noticed and accepted by NASA?

5. Music was still important to Ellen. She even played the flute onboard the Discovery spacecraft. What adjustments did she have to make to be able to do this?

6. Ellen was the world's first Latinx in space. Why do you think this is important?

7. Name some of Ellen's accomplishments during her four space missions.

8. There were many firsts for Ellen. Name some of them.

9. What do you think helped Ellen to become successful?

Select related children's literature

Jaffe, Elizabeth. *Ellen Ochoa*. New York: Children's Press, 2004.

Mahalia Jackson

by Nina Nolan   Grades 2–5

Summary

A beautifully illustrated book about how Mahalia
Jackson's music was the centerpiece of her life. She was
devoted to her family and often had to stop working to
take care of a sick relative. Through all this, the gospel
music she sang lifted her spirits and those of all who
heard her – thousands over her lifetime. Her aunt told
her that, "One day you'll walk with kings and queens"
(page 6). Read the story to find out how Mahalia did
this.

Nolan, Nina. *Mahalia Jackson*. New York: Amistad, 2015.

Questions for discussion, written responses, and/or research

1. Throughout her life, Mahalia sang gospel music.
What type of music is this?

2. What do you think her Aunt Bell meant when she
said to Mahalia, "One day you'll walk with kings
and queens"?

3. Mahalia did much of her singing in church. How did she support herself?

4. When Mahalia was sixteen, she went with her Aunt Hannah to Chicago. What did Mahalia hope to find in Chicago?

5. When her Aunt Hannah got sick, Mahalia had to work again, but did not give up her singing. She went to nightclubs to listen to bands play. Mahalia made a promise to God. What was this promise? Why did she make it?

6. Even though she was told by many people that she could make money in nightclubs, Mahalia only sang in churches. Why did she do this?

7. When Mahalia raised enough money for singing lessons, she was told by her teacher to stop singing so loudly. Why did Mahalia continue to sing in a loud voice?

8. Everyone noticed Mahalia's voice. She was signed by Decca Records to record a gospel album. How did this make her even more famous?

9. Mahalia sang at Carnegie Hall. Where is Carnegie Hall? What is it?

10. As she became more famous, who did she sing for?

11. What was the March on Washington? When did it occur? Who made the famous "I Have a Dream" speech?

Select related children's literature

Pinkney, Andrea Davis and Pinkney, Brian. *Martin and Mahalia: His Words, Her Song.* New York: Little, Brown and Company Books for Young Readers, 2013.

Ryan, Pam Muñoz. *When Marian Sang.* New York: Scholastic, 2002.

Vegara, Maria Isabel Sanchez. *Aretha Franklin.* London: Frances Lincoln Children's Books, 2020.

Weatherford, Carole Boston. *RESPECT: Aretha Franklin, The Queen of Soul.* New York: Atheneum Books for Young Readers, 2020.

Molly, By Golly!

by Dianne Ochiltree   Grades K–4

Summary

Molly Williams, born around 1818, was a slave in New York City. Her master was Benjamin Aymar, who was connected to the Fire Company Number 11, also in the city. Molly cooked for the firefighters in this company. One day a fire broke out in the neighborhood and many of the firefighters were sick with the flu, so Molly stepped up to the plate by spreading the news in the neighborhood and enlisting the help of its people in fighting the fire. She became a member of the fire company and helped put out the fire. For this, she is remembered as being the first African-American female firefighter in the United States.

Ochiltree, Dianne. *Molly, by Golly!* New York: Calkins Creek, 2012.

Questions for discussion, written responses, and/or research

1. Molly was a slave owned by Benjamin Aymar. Her main job was to cook for the firefighters in

Company 11. She was an excellent cook. What types of food did she make for the firefighters?

2. One day, Molly heard a fire alarm. Knowing that many of Company 11's firefighters were sick with the flu, Molly decided to help fight the fire. How did she notify the neighborhood of the fire?

3. How did the neighbors react?

4. How did Molly participate herself in putting out the fire?

5. What was on fire? What challenges were there to putting out the fire?

6. Roughly how long did it take to put out the fire?

7. What did you learn from this story?

Standing On Her Shoulders: A Celebration Of Women

by Monica Clark Robinson   Grades 3–8

Summary

This book, written as a poem, discusses the important accomplishments of the many women who came before us. Students will recognize some of these women from the illustrations and learn about others from their discussion of the story. The diverse women in the story and their achievements are highlighted at the end of the book. A great book to celebrate Black History Month.

Robinson, Monica Clark. *Standing on Her Shoulders: A Celebration of Women.* New York: Orchard Books, 2021.

Questions for discussion, written responses, and/or research

1. The story begins with the phrase, "You come from a deep, deep well" (page 2). What does this expression mean to you?

2. From reading this book, what do you think the expression, "standing on the shoulders of the strong, smart, sage and soulful ones who have come before us" (page 5) means?

3. Who are some of the women in your family on whose shoulders you will stand? What are some of their accomplishments?

4. Who are some of the women you recognize from the illustrations? What did each one accomplish? Notice the diversity in these women.

5. Who were some of the freedom seekers illustrated in the story? What did each of them do?

6. Who was one of the "brave and bold" bus riders whose shoulders we stand on? What did she do? How did she affect the future of African-American people?

7. Name some of the athletes shown in the illustrations? Which sport did each one represent?

8. What type of diversity is depicted in the illustrations of women in the book and in the story?

9. The book ends with, "Who will stand on YOURS?" (page 31). Who will stand on your shoulders? Explain your answer.

10. The women in the story include Serena Williams, Shirley Chisholm, Deb Haaland, Frida Kahlo, Hilary Clinton, Mary Cassatt, Sacajawea, and Zora Neal Thurston. Google one of these women to find out who she was and what she accomplished for us to stand on her shoulders.

Select related children's literature

Kudlinski, Kathleen. *Rosa Parks.* New York: Aladdin, 2001.

Levy, Debbie. *I Dissent: Ruth Bader Ginsburg Makes Her Mark.* New York: Simon and Schuster, 2016.

Moss, Caroline. *Become a Leader Like Michelle Obama.* Minneapolis: Frances Lincoln Children's Books, 2020.

Vegara, Maria Isabel Sanchez. *Frida Kahlo.* London: Frances Lincoln Children's Books, 2016.

When Marian Sang

by Pam Muñoz Ryan   Grades 4–8

Summary

Marian Anderson sang throughout her life. As she sought to enroll in formal voice lessons and to perform in public, she encountered obstacles because of the color of her skin. This book chronicles her journey to becoming one of the most famous opera singers in the world in the twentieth century.

Ryan, Pam Muñoz. *When Marian Sang*. New York: Scholastic, 2002.

Questions for discussion, written responses, and/or research

1. Who inspired Marian to sing?

2. Marian's choir director, Alexander Robinson, wanted her, at only eight years old, to harmonize with a friend as they sang a duet. What is a duet? What does harmonize mean?

3. Marian had a beautiful voice from a young age. When she sang, she frequently closed her eyes. Why did she do this?

4. Where was Marian born and raised? In what year was she born? Where can you find this information in the book?

5. How was Marian able to raise the tuition fees for music school? How could her church members support her?

6. What made Marian feel "invisible" when she tried to apply to music school?

7. What is prejudice? How did Marian experience prejudice in her lifetime? Have you ever experienced prejudice? In what ways? What can we do as a society to combat this?

8. Outline some of Marian's hopes and dreams.

9. Eventually, Marian was given an audition with a famous singer, who had claimed he had no time or room for a new student. What did Marian do to convince this teacher? Why do you think this was a good idea?

10. Why did Marian travel to Europe to sing?

11. When Marian returned to the United States in the late 1930s, she once again faced prejudice. What, in particular, happened to her? How did people support Marian as she tried to deal with this prejudice?

12. For the next sixteen years, after the Lincoln Memorial performance, Marian "sang for kings and queens, presidents and prime ministers, famous composers and conductors" (page 28). When and where did Marian finally reach the "sun and the moon" (page 29)?

Select related children's literature

Weatherford, Carole Boston. *Leontyne Price.* New York: Alfred Knopf, 2014.

Hidden Figures

by Margot Lee Shetterly   Grades 3–8

Summary

Who are Dorothy Vaughan, Mary Jackson, Katherine Johnson, and Christine Darden? *Hidden Figures* is a story, made into a movie, about four African-American mathematicians who grew up facing racism and discrimination as they strived to become computers – the human kind. While in modern-day society computers are powerful machines, in the mid-twentieth century computers were human. These women made great impacts on the space industry, despite the many racial challenges they faced.

Shetterly, Margot Lee. *Hidden Figures: The True Story of Four Black Women and the Space Race.* New York: HarperCollins, 2018.

Questions for discussion, written responses, and/or research

1. What were some of the challenges Dorothy Vaughan faced as she tried to get a job as a mathematical computer?

2. Once she was offered a position as a computer at Langley Laboratory in Hampton, Virginia, what were some of the things Dorothy couldn't do with her white counterparts?

3. Mary Jackson also worked at Langley. What job did she have?

4. Mary was discouraged from becoming an engineer. What were some of the obstacles she faced? How was she able to overcome them and become the first African-American woman engineer at Langley?

5. Katherine Johnson, who was also great at math, participated in research to determine what potential problems turbulence could cause for a plane. What is turbulence? What did Katherine and the researchers conclude?

6. How did Katherine's persistence result in her becoming part of this research group?

7. In the 1950s Langley purchased a computer machine which could calculate faster than any human. Why did Dorothy have to monitor the computer calculations?

8. What is NASA? What do the letters mean?

9. Why was NASA formed from the National Advisory Committee for Aeronautics? Which country was the United States in competition with?

10. President John Fitzgerald Kennedy had a goal to land a man on the moon before the end of the 1960s.

What did NASA have to do before this could be accomplished? Why was this so important?

11. What was Katherine Johnson's role in getting an astronaut into space?

12. Racial discrimination began to lessen in the 1960s. What were some of the things African Americans and whites could now do?

13. Christine Darden worked well with computers – the electronic kind. How did it become possible for her to become an engineer in the late 1960s?

14. In 1969, the United States landed its first astronaut on the moon. Why was this a "giant leap for mankind" (page 28) and a great accomplishment for the female computers and engineers who had worked at Langley and NASA for so many years?

15. Do some research on each of the four Hidden Figures – Dorothy Vaughan, Mary Jackson, Katherine Johnson, and Christine Darden. Mary Jackson died in 2005, but it was only recently that an honor was bestowed on her. What was this honor? Did the four ladies know each other?

16. Explore the resources at the end of the book – a timeline of the aeronautics industry, short biographies of the four women, and a glossary of aeronautical terms.

Select related children's literature

Becker, Helaine. *Counting on Katherine: How Katherine Johnson Saved Apollo 13.* New York: Henry Holt and Company, 2018.

Diehn, Andi. *Computer Decoder: Dorothy Vaughan.* White River Junction, VT: Nomad Press, 2019.

Aretha Franklin

by Maria Isabel Sanchez Vegara   Grades 4–8

Summary

Aretha Franklin was born to sing. Her parents separated when she was young and she began touring with her father, a preacher, from church to church. Singing beautiful gospel music, she longed to sing for the public, and her dream became a reality when she received her first record contract. From there, her singing career took off.

Vegara, Maria Isabel Sanchez. *Aretha Franklin*. London: Frances Lincoln Children's Books, 2020.

Questions for discussion, written responses, and/or research

1. What and who inspired Aretha to sing?

2. List some of the ways Aretha was surrounded by music as she was growing up.

3. Her career took off once she was offered a record contract. What was her most popular song? What important message did it carry? Who wrote this song for her to perform?

4. Aretha was also a songwriter. Which types of music did she write?

5. What was the theme in most of the songs Aretha wrote?

6. How long did it take Aretha to be inducted into the Rock & Roll Hall of Fame?

7. Why was Aretha a trailblazer for many female artists?

8. Aretha sang at the inauguration of the first African-American president of the United States. What is his name? In which year was he inaugurated?

9. Google soul music and discuss what you found out with your class.

Select related children's literature

Weatherford, Carole Boston. *RESPECT: Aretha Franklin, The Queen of Soul.* New York: Atheneum Books for Young Readers, 2020.

Leontyne Price

by Carole Boston Weatherford   Grades 4–8

Summary

Born in 1927 to a midwife and a sawmill worker, Leontyne's hopes and dreams to be an opera singer were obstructed by racism. Despite this, with her journey to stardom paved by Marian Anderson, Leontyne was able to fulfill her dreams.

Weatherford, Carole Boston. *Leontyne Price*. New York: Alfred Knopf, 2014.

Questions for discussion, written responses, and/or research

1. What inspired Leontyne to sing?

2. What did her parents do to help her face the obstacles of racism?

3. How did her parents bring music into their home?

4. In which ways was Leontyne influenced by Marian Anderson?

5. How were Marian Anderson and Leontyne Price alike?

6. Leontyne went to college with the intention of becoming a teacher. Why did she give up her dream of singing? What changed her mind?

7. What was Leontyne's first major performance?

8. When her opera career opened up, which roles did she perform?

9. Despite her groundbreaking performances, she was still unable to do many of the things white people could do. What were some of those things?

10. Through which medium did Leontyne become well known?

11. Leontyne was most famous for her portrayal of Aida, an Ethiopian princess. The book says, "Leontyne stood on Marian's shoulders" (page 26). What does this phrase mean?

12. Where and what is Julliard? You may have to do some research to find out.

13. Leontyne performed at the Metropolitan Opera House in New York City in 1955. She received a forty-two-minute standing ovation. Who did she credit with her success as she tearfully listened to the applause?

14. Make a Venn diagram using words that show how Leontyne Price and Marian Anderson were alike (eg. where they were born and where they performed etc.). Then write a short essay comparing the two opera singers.

Select related children's literature

Ryan, Pam Muñoz. *When Marian Sang*. New York: Scholastic, 2002.

The Legendary Miss Lena Horne

by Carole Boston Weatherford   Grades 5–8

Summary

The book begins with a quote from Lena Horne: "You have to be taught to be second class; you're not born that way" (page v). Born in 1917, during the beginning of the Harlem Renaissance, Lena Horne was an actress, singer, and civil rights activist who came from a family of achievers. Her father was a gambler and her mother an aspiring actress. Becoming the poster child of the NAACP at only two years old, Lena faced racism in all aspects of her life. From not being allowed to try on shoes because she was black, to singing with a white band but not being allowed to enter the theater through the front door because she was black, to being labeled as a Cuban so she wouldn't face black discrimination, she was the NAACP's role model for helping to change the ways blacks were perceived and treated. The story and illustrations are beautiful, depicting the life of Miss Horne.

Weatherford, Carole Boston. *The Legendary Miss Lena Horne*. New York: Atheneum Books for Young Readers, 2017.

Questions for discussion, written response and/or research

1. What was the Harlem Renaissance? When did it occur? What happened during this Renaissance? You may have to do some research on these questions.

2. What did Lena's father and mother do to make a living? Why did they go their separate ways when Lena was just a toddler?

3. Lena's picture was on the front page of the NAACP's bulletin when she was just two years old. What is the NAACP?

4. Lena stayed with her grandmother when her parents left. What values did Lena's grandmother instill in her at a young age?

5. Why did Lena's grandmother not want her to be a show-business entertainer?

6. What were some racist things that happened to Lena and other blacks once she began traveling with her mother again?

7. She returned to stay with her grandmother and attended an integrated all-girls school. What does integrated mean?

8. When did Lena finally go on stage? What was the reason?

9. What was the Cotton Club? What racist incidents did Lena face at the Cotton Club?

10. Where did black performers stay after their shows? Why was this?

11. What other racial incidents did Lena encounter when she toured with an all-white big band?

12. What were the goals of the NAACP with respect to Lena?

13. What discrimination did black moviegoers face when they went to a theater to see Lena perform in a film?

14. What steps did Lena take to rise above the indignity shown to black women?

15. Lena married, had two children, and divorced. She later remarried a white man, but had to keep the marriage hidden for three years. What was the reason?

16. What does the book describe as Lena's most important work of her lifetime? When did this occur?

17. Which honors and awards did Lena earn during her lifetime? Research each of these.

Select related children's literature

Haquet, Alice Brière. *Nina*. Watertown, MA: Charlesbridge, 2017.

Voice Of Freedom: Fannie Lou Hamer

by Carole Boston Weatherford   Grades 4–8

Summary

Beautifully illustrated and written, this book is a chronology written in a poetic form of prose about the life of civil rights activist Fannie Lou Hamer. She was the twentieth child of sharecroppers who, along with her parents and nineteen siblings, worked in the cotton fields. Realizing that her family lived in poverty, she wanted to know why she wasn't white so she could have "food, clothing, and everything" (page 5). The book can be read in parts and details the strife Fannie Lou's family endured and her subsequent accomplishments.

Weatherford, Carole Boston. *Voice of Freedom: Fannie Lou Hamer*. Somerville, MA: Candlewick Press, 2015.

Questions for discussion, written responses, and/or research

1. Fannie Lou was the youngest of twenty children. Her family worked in the cotton fields. How old was Fannie when she started to work in the cotton fields?

2. For how many hours a day did her family work? What were the conditions like?

3. Why wasn't her family paid fairly? What did Fannie compare sharecropping to? Why did she say this?

4. How did her mother provide clothes for the family?

5. What did Fannie's mother do when Fannie compared herself to white people? Why do you think she did this?

6. When did Fannie and her siblings go to school? Why was this time chosen for kids to attend school?

7. How were black people portrayed in the textbooks used at school? How did Fannie feel about this?

8. Describe the family's living conditions.

9. Her father finally raised enough money to buy a wagon, some mules, and cows. What happened to his purchases? Why?

10. Why did much of Fannie's family move to the North?

11. What was Jim Crow? You may have to research this to find the information you need.

12. When the master cheated the sharecroppers by weighing the cotton incorrectly, how did Fannie try to right this wrong?

13. Fannie married Perry Hamer. How did they make a living?

14. Why couldn't Fannie have babies of her own? What did she and her husband do to have a family?

15. Why was it difficult for Fannie to earn the right to vote? When did Fannie get this right? Which of the obstacles that stood in her way did she overcome?

16. Fannie Lou Hamer became a civil rights activist. One of the things she and people she trained with at citizenship school did was to sit at a white lunch counter at a bus terminal. What happened to Fannie after the police were called? How did Fannie get through this terrible ordeal?

17. What were the lasting effects of her imprisonment on Fannie?

18. Fannie ran for political office several times but did not get elected. What was her reason for running?

19. What was the Ku Klux Klan? What did they stand for? Do they still exist today?

20. Fannie visited Guinea with a famous singer. Who was the singer and what was the purpose of her visit? Locate Guinea on a map. Which continent is it located on?

21. What were some of the things Fannie did for black people when she returned to the United States?

22. What did Fannie identify as America's problem? How is it still a problem today? What types of things can we do to overcome this problem?

Select related children's literature

Alexander, Kwame. *The Undefeated.* New York: Houghton Mifflin Harcourt, 2019.

Asim, Jabari. *A Child's Introduction to African American History.* New York: Black Dog and Leventhal Publishers, 2018.

Sonia Sotomayor

by Jonah Winter   Grades K–6

Summary

This book describes the life of Sonia Sotomayor, who ultimately became a Supreme Court Justice and has served on the bench since 2009. Sonia Sotomayor grew up in South Bronx, New York. Her family was poor and her mother worked hard to be able to send Sonia and her brother to private schools. Sonia's father had died when she was nine. The book is written in both English and Spanish, with the Spanish below the English.

Winter, Jonah. *Sonia Sotomayor.* New York: Atheneum Books for Young Readers, 2009.

Questions for discussion, written responses, and/or research

1. Discuss Sonia's childhood. What did she like to do? Besides working so hard, what did her mother like to do? What did she want to become? Why?

2. The story states that, "Her [Sonia's] blossoming began with her mother's love and hard work" (page 4). In what ways did Sonia "blossom" throughout her life?

3. Where were Sonia's parents from? What aspects of the culture from their homeland did Sonia enjoy? What traditions did her family and friends have?

4. Name some of the books Sonia read. How did these books inspire Sonia to always do her best?

5. What type of student was Sonia? Where did she go to college? Why did she feel so isolated during her college years?

6. In which ways did Sonia face discrimination?

7. List some things her classmates did that Sonia couldn't do. How did this make her feel?

8. Sonia was determined to thrive during college. What types of things did she do despite the discrimination she faced?

9. What type of leadership role did she take in college? Why was this so important to her and to those who looked like her?

10. How did her life affect her as a judge?

11. Which president nominated her for the Supreme Court? In which year?

12. Why was it so important that Sonia be on the Supreme Court?

Select related children's literature

Jeffrey, Gary. *Thurgood Marshall: The Supreme Court Rules on "Separate but Equal"*. New York: Gareth Stevens Publishing, 2013.

Rhodes-Pitts, Sharifa. *Jake Makes a World*. New York: MoMA, 2015.

Sanders, Joshunda. *I Can Write the World*. Houston: Six Foot Press, 2019.

Woodson, Jacqueline. *The Day You Begin*. New York: Nancy Paulson, 2018.

PART FOUR

DIVERSE MALE ACHIEVERS

Birth Of The Cool

by Kathleen Cornell Berman   Grades 4–8

Summary

This book chronicles the musical life of Miles Davis from age six to twenty-nine. Miles heard music in everything and from an early age worked to craft his unique sound, which he learned from the great musicians such as Louis Armstrong, Duke Ellington, and his great teacher, Elwood Buchanan. Miles also encountered racism, but overcame this to become one of the greatest jazz trumpeters of all time.

Berman, Kathleen Cornell. *Birth of the Cool.* Salem, MA: Page Street Kids, 2019.

Questions for discussion, written responses, and/or research

1. Miles was a well-rounded young child. His foremost love was music, but he also did other activities. Name some of these things.

2. Why did Miles spend a lot of time near the Mississippi River, which was close to his home?

3. Which musician was a great influence on Miles, even at a young age?

4. Miles spent his summers with his grandpa in Arkansas. How did Miles find music there?

5. Miles received a bright new trumpet when he was thirteen. How did he learn to play the trumpet so well?

6. Although his playing became great, Miles did not win prizes in competitive performances. Why? What was his reaction and his resolve?

7. Miles grew his music with the times. What was Bebop, which Miles began playing?

8. Which musicians began to influence Miles at this point in his life?

9. Although he dropped out, Miles went to a famous music school in New York City. What was the name of this school? Why did he drop out? Who was he looking for in New York City?

10. What advice did Miles's father give him when he dropped out of music school?

11. When Dizzy Gillespie dropped out of Charlie "Bird" Parker's Band, Miles stepped into his place. What difficulties did he encounter playing in Bird's band?

12. What advice did Bird give him when Miles was ready to quit the band?

13. Miles was looking for a new way to play his trumpet. How did he prepare for doing this?

14. Miles became a leader of his own group of musicians. His band was called a nonet. What does that mean?

15. This book is entitled *Birth of the Cool*. What was "cool" about Miles's band?

16. What does the expression "the trumpet is his voice" (page 31) mean as it relates to Miles?

Select related children's literature

Andrews, Troy. *Trombone Shorty*. New York: Abrams, 2015.

McDonough, Yona Zeldis. *Who Was Louis Armstrong?* New York: Penguin Random House, 2004.

Orgill, Roxanne. *If I Only Had a Horn*. Boston: Houghton Mifflin Harcourt, 1997.

Pinkney, Andrea Davis. *Duke Ellington*. New York: Hyperion, 1998.

Russell-Brown, Katheryn. *Little Melba and Her Big Trombone*. New York: Lee and Low, 2014.

Lin-Manuel Miranda

by Laurie Calkhoven   **Grades 2–5**

Summary

Lin-Manuel Miranda is an American singer, playwright, actor, director, producer, and songwriter. This multitalented son of Puerto Rican parents grew up with music in his home and neighborhood, which was mostly Hispanic. He was a big fan of Disney movies – he and his wife even named their first son Sebastian after a character from *The Little Mermaid*. At the end of the book there is a short history of Puerto Rico, and fun facts about Broadway and its theaters and shows, especially the ones in which Lin-Manuel was involved.

Calkhoven, Laurie. *Lin-Manuel Miranda*. New York: Simon Spotlight, 2018.

Questions for discussion, written responses, and/or research

1. This book about the life and accomplishments of Lin-Manuel Miranda is divided into five chapters. Read one chapter a day and discuss the accomplishments of Lin-Manuel Miranda throughout his life to date.

2. Explore the interesting information at the end of the book, which includes fun facts about Broadway and its theaters and shows, and a brief history of Puerto Rico.

Carter Reads The Newspaper

by Deborah Hopkinson   Grades 4–6

Summary

Carter Woodson founded Black History Month, originally called Black History Week, selecting the week when both Abraham Lincoln and Frederick Douglass were born. Mostly self-educated throughout his young life, Carter worked hard in the coal mines to earn money for his family. At age twenty, he went to high school and completed his studies in two years. He continued his studies at college, where he earned a Master's Degree. At the age of thirty-seven he earned a Ph.D. from Harvard University – the first African American born of slaves to earn this degree. The story is full of important African-American achievers, who are listed and pictured throughout the book, and provides a meaningful basis for discussing the significance of Black History Month.

Hopkinson, Deborah. *Carter Reads the Newspaper.* Atlanta: Peachtree, 2019.

Questions for discussion, written responses, and/or research

1. Carter's family was poor, his parents having been freed slaves. How did his family care for each other and put food on the table?

2. Where did Carter acquire the newspapers he read to his father to keep him up to date?

3. What kinds of jobs did Carter have to help support his family before he attended high school at age twenty?

4. In which ways did Oliver Jones contribute to the education of Carter and Oliver's friends?

5. How was Carter Woodson inspired by Oliver Jones? How did this contribute to both their educations?

6. Carter created Black History Week in 1926. When did the United States create Black History Month, celebrated in February of each year?

7. How do you celebrate Black History Month? Who are some of the people and what are some of the achievements you celebrate?

8. Carter had a history professor who claimed that blacks had no history. What did Carter do to prove him wrong? Name some of the ways he got information to the people.

9. The book ends with the line, "Carter G. Woodson didn't just study history. He changed it. And we can too" (page 27). How did Carter Woodson change history? How can we continue his work?

10. Many African-American achievers are mentioned and/or pictured in the book. They include famous people and those who are less known to the general public. Do some research on the lesser-known people, including Carter G. Woodson, Oliver Jones, W.E.B. Du Bois, Lewis Latimer, Ida B. Wells, Sarah Breedlove, Colin Kaepernick, and Richard Wright. Many others are referenced in the book. Select one and google them. Work in pairs to prepare a short oral presentation on your findings to the class.

Select related children's literature

Engle, Susan. *Robert Sengstacke Abbott: A Man, a Paper, and a Parade.* Wilmette, IL: Bellwood, 2019.

I Promise

by LeBron James   **Grades K–4**

Summary

LeBron James was motivated to write this book as a result of opening the I Promise School in Akron, Ohio. The I Promise School is a public school that admits at-risk students through a lottery system. The school has been open for nearly three years and the students are making academic progress as well as learning important life skills. The book is uplifting and motivates each of its readers to be the best that they can be.

James, LeBron. *I Promise*. New York: HarperCollins, 2020.

Questions for discussion, written responses, and/or research

1. Stop after reading each pair of pages and think about what is meant by the promise stated on the page. How does each illustration support the words? For example, some questions for the third and fourth pages of the book might be:

– How does the illustration show that the students are following the rules?

– How does the illustration show children reading as much as they can?

2. There are many figurative expressions in the book. As you read each one, discuss its meaning in relation to the story. For example, what does the phrase "I promise to run full court and show up each time" (page 5) mean in the context of the story?

3. How does the illustration on pages 9 and 10 show the students are accepting defeat with "strength and humility"?

4. Why is it important to ask for help when needed? How does the illustration on the page on which this is discussed indicate help is needed?

5. How do the illustrations in the rest of the book support the text?

Select related children's literature

Barnes, Derrick and James, Gordon C. *I Am Every Good Thing.* New York: Penguin Random House, 2020.

Byers, Grace. *I Am Enough.* New York: Balzer and Bray, 2018.

Byers, Grace. *I Believe I Can.* New York: Balzer and Bray, 2020.

Dream Builder: The Story Of Architect Philip Freelon

by Kelly Starling Lyons   Grades 2–6

Summary

Philip Freelon, a Philadelphian, was a contemporary architect. Coming from a family of artists, educators, and business people, he had an early interest in drawing. Though he had difficulty in learning to read, he soared in STEAM (Science, Technology, Engineering, Art, and Math) subjects as he grew up. He had many positive influences in his life, but also confronted racial injustice and prejudice. *Dream Builder* chronicles the life, accomplishments, and challenges of Philip Freelon as he became one of the great architects of all time.

Lyons, Kelly Starling. *Dream Builder: The Story of Architect Philip Freelon*. New York: Lee and Low, 2020.

Questions for discussion, written responses, and/or research

1. As Philip's interest in drawing and sculpture grew, what kinds of projects did he do?

2. How did Philip's mind help him create his projects? Who inspired him to think deeply and use all his senses to discover nature? This is called an artist's inner eye. What do you think an inner eye means?

3. Though reading was difficult for him to master, how did Philip eventually learn to read? How did his love of art help him?

4. What were some of the racial prejudices Philip confronted?

5. Philip was proud of his neighborhood. How does he describe it?

6. Where did Philip go to high school? In drafting class, what unique ability does Philip demonstrate when asked to look at the front of a machine and then draw the whole machine, including all four sides?

7. Which subjects were not included in the architecture program Philip studied at university?

8. Philip Freelon designed places that would help people. What types of buildings did he design?

9. Have you ever visited Washington, D.C.? Which buildings or landmarks did you visit? What did you notice about them?

10. Why do you think the book is titled *Dream Builder*?

11. Philip was asked to be part of a team of architects charged with the design of a museum to celebrate African-American history and culture. The museum was completed before President Barack Obama, the first black president of the United States, completed his second presidential term and is part of the Smithsonian Institution in Washington, D.C. Which other museums are part of the Smithsonian Institution? What else is located in Washington, D.C.? In pairs, use Google to find out.

12. Philip's grandfather was a well-known painter of the Harlem Renaissance. Work in pairs to google the Harlem Renaissance and then discuss your findings as a class.

Jake Makes A World

by Sharifa Rhodes-Pitts　　　　　Grades 3–8

Summary

This beautifully illustrated book tells the story of the Harlem Renaissance painter, Jacob Lawrence. Jake painted scenes from life in Harlem, where he lived from the age of thirteen. He also painted scenes from the Great Migration of 1917 to 1970, when African Americans moved to the North to escape the racial discrimination and segregation of the rural South.

Rhodes-Pitts, Sharifa. *Jake Makes a World*. New York: MoMA, 2015.

Questions for discussion, written responses, and/or research

1. As you read the book, discuss some of the city scenes that Jacob painted.

2. Where did Jake learn to paint? What other art forms did he create?

3. Jake creates a diorama of a street in Harlem using a shoebox. Where is Harlem? What did he include in his diorama?

4. Research the Harlem Renaissance and discuss what you find out with the class.

5. Research the Migration Series. When did Jacob Lawrence paint this series? How many paintings does it include? Where are they housed today?

6. Why is the book entitled *Jake Makes a World*?

Before John Was A Jazz Giant

by Carole Boston Weatherford   Grades K–4

Summary

Before John Coltrane became a well-known jazz musician, he heard music in everyday things – in the birds singing, in the preacher giving a sermon, from Grandma's phonograph, in tap dancing, on the radio. He continued listening until one day he picked up a horn and started making his own music, becoming a famous saxophonist in the early 1960s.

Weatherford, Carole Boston. *Before John Was a Jazz Giant*. New York: Henry Holt and Company, 2008.

Questions for discussion, written responses, and/or research

1. John was born into a musical family. How were each of his parents involved with music?

2. John heard music in all of nature's sounds. Name some of these sounds.

3. John heard music in tap dancers and jitterbuggers. What is a tap dance? What is the jitterbug?

4. Do you think John Coltrane taught himself to play the saxophone? Give reasons for your answer.

5. How was John involved with music in high school? You can find information on this in the author's note at the end of the book.

6. What caused him to risk his life while playing music?

7. Why is John Coltrane called a jazz legend?

Select related children's literature

Andrews, Troy. *Trombone Shorty.* New York: Abrams, 2015.

Orgill, Roxanne. *If I Only Had a Horn.* Boston: Houghton Mifflin Harcourt, 1997.

Pinkney, Andrea Davis. *Duke Ellington.* New York: Hyperion, 1998.

Russell-Brown, Katheryn. *Little Melba and Her Big Trombone.* New York: Lee and Low, 2014.

Gordon Parks

by Carole Boston Weatherford   Grades K–4

Summary

Gordon Parks faced racism as a young student, from a teacher who told her black students that they would all become "porters and waiters." Coming from a family of fifteen children and losing his mother at age fifteen, Gordon had different ideas about his future. Inspired to buy a used camera when he was twenty-five, he taught himself how to take great photographs and eventually had his first exhibition at a camera store. Gordon went on to become an official photographer in Washington, D.C., where he saw many disparities between the ways white and black people lived. He continued to use a camera to tell stories of racism throughout his life, becoming the first black photographer for two major U.S. magazines.

Weatherford, Carole Boston. *Gordon Parks.* Chicago: Albert Whitman, 2015.

Questions for discussion, written responses, and/or research

1. How does the author define segregation?

2. In what ways did Gordon face racism in his young adult years?

3. Gordon took pictures of struggling families in Chicago, after which he worked as a photographer for a company in Washington, D.C. What advice did his boss give him about what to take pictures of?

4. As he traveled around Washington, what types of things and people did Gordon see? How did this affect the photos he would take?

5. What did Gordon learn about going into stores in Washington, D.C.?

6. Gordon went to his boss for advice about how he could expose racism with his camera. What advice did his boss give him? Why do you think this was good advice?

7. Who was Ella Watson? What made her so special? How did Gordon Parks learn so much from her?

8. Gordon's most famous photo is entitled "American Gothic." What did this photo portray?

9. What else did Gordon Parks accomplish?

10. What did you learn from the story of Gordon Parks?

Schomburg: The Man Who Built A Library

by Carole Boston Weatherford   Grades 6–8

Summary

The book opens with a quote by Arturo Schomburg: "The American Negro must remake his past in order to make his future. History must restore what slavery took away," (page ii) and describes in detail the life of Arturo Schomburg, an African Puerto Rican American, a bibliophile, collector, and historian. Devoting his life to making the achievements of African Americans known, especially those who rose from slavery, he was an important person in the Harlem Renaissance. Because it is so richly detailed, the book lends itself to being read one or two pages at a time to a child or class.

Weatherford, Carole Boston. *Schomburg: The Man Who Built a Library.* Somerville, MA: Candlewick Press, 2017.

Questions for discussion, written responses, and/or research

Fifth Grade

1. How did Arturo learn to read as a young boy?

2. What was Arturo's reaction when his fifth-grade teacher told him the people of Africa had no history?

Genius

3. Arturo was not satisfied with his fifth-grade teacher's declaration that the people of Africa had no history. What were some of the things he did as a young boy in the quest for African history?

4. Who was Benjamin Banneker? What did Banneker do? Were his accomplishments recognized?

El Immigrante / The Immigrant

5. How old was Schomburg when he immigrated to New York?

6. How did he introduce himself to the people of New York?

7. How did Arturo learn to speak English? How did he earn an income when he arrived in New York?

8. Though he had a formal education in Puerto Rico, he could not pursue studies in medicine and law. Why?

9. What remarkable accomplishment did Arturo achieve to protect the Johnson and Johnson red logo on its products?

The Book Hunting Bug

10. Arturo started searching for books about contributions made by Africans. Where did he find these books?

11. Who was Phillis Wheatley? What did she accomplish?

12. What happened to the second manuscript she wrote?

Frederick Douglass

13. Who was Frederick Douglass? What were some of his accomplishments?

14. What was the name of Douglass's antislavery newspaper?

Revolutionaries

15. Arturo began collecting more than just books to help raise awareness of African history and accomplishments. Why was Toussaint Louverture a hero to Arturo?

16. What was the Haitian revolution?

17. Who was David Walker and what did he publish? For what purpose?

18. Who was Nat Turner? What did he incite? Why?

Three Elizabeths

19. How many wives did Schomburg have? What were their names?

20. How many children did Schomburg have?

21. Why did he not allow any of his children to learn Spanish?

Whitewash

22. What did Arturo suspect about the cause of ignorance of African history?

23. Who was Alexandre Dumas? Google Dumas to find more about him and what his nationality was.

24. Who was Alexander Pushkin? What was his nationality? What was he known for?

25. Who was Ludwig van Beethoven? What ties did he have to Africa?

Seafaring

26. Arturo collected books from Paul Cuffee. Who was he? What was he famous for?

Bloodhound

27. Arturo met Alain Locke. Who was he?

28. Who was Booker T. Washington? What was he known for?

29. W.E.B. Du Bois was a famous African American. What was his major accomplishment?

30. What was the Harlem Renaissance? Name some of the writers of this era.

31. Schomburg had extensive booklists. What did he do with all his books?

Home

32. Schomburg's home was filled with books. How did his wife try to create a living space for the family? Was she successful?

33. Why did Fernando Schomburg say his father was always so busy?

Writer And Researcher

34. In what ways did Schomburg immerse himself in the history of Africa for the world to be informed?

35. What types of things did Schomburg do to keep busy?

36. What was the diaspora? Use Google to find out information about it.

37. What was the article "The Negro Digs Up His Past," written by Schomburg, about?

Sold

38. What did Schomburg eventually do with his extensive collection of books?

39. What was included in Schomburg's collection? Where was his vast library stored?

40. Name some famous writers whose works were part of Schomburg's collection.

41. Use Google to find out where his collection is today.

Fisk University

42. Schomburg was a bibliophile. What do you think this word means?

43. What was Schomburg's connection with Fisk University in Nashville, Tennessee?

44. What did Schomburg tell the Fisk University professors to teach?

Doctor

45. How did Schomburg catalogue his books at the 135th Street branch of the New York Public Library?

46. What is meant by the expression on page 34, "Tell our stories, proclaim our glories"?

47. Who called Arturo "Dr. Schomburg"? Why did they give him that title?

Art

48. What was Schomburg's purpose in collecting art?

49. List some of the painters whose art he collected.

Spain

50. What was Schomburg's purpose in traveling to Spain? Why did he feel it was time to do this?

51. While visiting Spain, he also visited other European countries. What were some of these countries? What was the purpose of his visits?

The Islands

52. Where did Schomburg's continued research take him?

53. What was the result of his visit to these countries?

Epitaph 1938

54. Having read the story, why do you think the proverb "A book is like a garden carried in a pocket" is applicable to Schomburg?

Timeline At The End Of The Book

55. Review the timeline at the end of the book for valuable information on milestones in Schomburg's life.

Thurgood

by Jonah Winter   Grades 4–8

Summary

This book chronicles the life of Thurgood Marshall from a toddler to a U.S. Supreme Court Justice. Even as a six-year-old child, he made a convincing argument to his parents to change his name from Thoroughgood to Thurgood. He faced racism in many ways and reacted by making the fight of racism part of his life's mission. The story is beautifully illustrated and is a great introduction to the life of this brilliant man.

Winter, Jonah. *Thurgood.* New York: Schwartz and Wade Books, 2019.

Questions for discussion, written responses, and/or research

1. Thurgood Marshall was arrested at fifteen years of age. What were the racially biased circumstances that led to his arrest?

2. How did racial bias present itself in the education system when Thurgood was in school? Describe the high school that Thurgood attended.

3. What did the phrase "separate but equal" refer to?

4. How does the author describe the world Thurgood lived in?

5. Thurgood's dad frequently took him to the courtroom to listen to trials, where lawyers argued their cases. What did his father want Thurgood to gain from listening to these trials?

6. How did his father follow up about the trials with Thurgood when they were at home? What was his father hoping to accomplish for Thurgood?

7. How did Thurgood highlight his speaking skills through high school and college?

8. Thurgood knew he wanted to become a lawyer in his senior year of college. What obstacles did he face when he applied to law school? When he eventually became a lawyer, what was his first major legal action? What was the outcome?

9. What is the NAACP and how was Thurgood involved with this organization?

10. Why did Thurgood fear for his life when he tried cases in the southern United States?

11. Why did Thurgood earn the name, "Mr. Civil Rights"?

12. Thurgood argued many cases in front of the United States Supreme Court. Write a summary of some of these cases and their outcomes.

13. What were Thurgood's feelings about segregating black students? What were the disadvantages to doing this, particularly when it came to schools?

14. Thurgood was appointed to be a Supreme Court Justice. He was the first black Supreme Court Justice. What obstacles to his appointment did he face? How long did he serve on the Supreme Court of the United States?

15. Jim Crow laws were enacted after the Civil War and continued well into the twentieth century. What were these laws? What was their purpose? Google to find out about Jim Crow laws.

Select related children's literature

Jeffrey, Gary. *Thurgood Marshall: The Supreme Court Rules on "Separate but Equal"*. New York: Gareth Stevens Publishing, 2013.

PART FIVE
INSPIRATIONAL CHILDREN

Dancing In The Wings

by Debbie Allen   Grades 2–5

Summary

This book by the famed dancer, choreographer, and actress, Debbie Allen, is based on her own experiences growing up as a dancer. The main character in the story is Sassy, who is tall, too tall she thinks for her life's ambition to be a ballerina. She also has big feet and is often the target of mean-spirited comments from her brother and other students. Read how she deals with some of the bullying and how her Uncle Redd gives her advice that allows her to achieve success as a dancer.

Allen, Debbie. *Dancing in the Wings*. New York: Puffin Books, 2000.

Questions for discussion, written responses, and/or research

1. Sassy was self-conscious about her height and the size of her feet. Kids made fun of her, which contributed to her self-consciousness. Which events in the story helped her regain her confidence?

2. How old do you think the children in the story were? Why do you think so?

3. How did Sassy's Uncle Redd help her recognize the gifts she had? What could she do that other children shorter than her could not do?

4. Why is the story titled *Dancing in the Wings*?

5. Since Sassy already stood out because of her height and large feet, what was her thinking in deciding to wear a yellow leotard to her audition for the summer program?

6. Each of us is different from every other person. Name some of these differences. Why should they be celebrated?

7. There are several ballet terms used in the story. Research what the following words mean: *tendu, solo, duet, tutu*. Do you take dance lessons? What are some other terms that are used and what do they mean?

Select related children's literature

Copeland, Misty. *Bunheads*. New York: Penguin Random House, 2020.

Pinkney, Andrea Davis. *Alvin Ailey*. Los Angeles: Hyperion, 1993.

Trombone Shorty

by Troy Andrews   Grades 1–5

Summary

The author, Troy Andrews, earned the nickname Trombone Shorty as a small child because the trombone he played was much larger than he was. There was always music playing in Treme, the neighborhood in New Orleans, Louisiana, where he grew up. Mardi Gras was Trombone Shorty's favorite time of the year. Bands marched down the street while people danced, and music sounded like gumbo – a mixture of many sounds of different styles. People made their own instruments and everyone had a great time. Read the book to find out how Shorty got his name and how he progressed to be the great musician he is today at the young age of thirty-five.

Andrews, Troy. *Trombone Shorty*. New York: Abrams, 2015.

Questions for discussion, written responses, and/or research

1. How did friends say hello to each other "New Orleans" style?

2. How did Troy Andrews get the nickname "Trombone Shorty"?

3. What are some of the sights and sounds of Mardi Gras, which is celebrated every year in New Orleans?

4. Shorty's older brother had a band, which Shorty and his friends wanted to join. Why do you think Shorty and his friends couldn't be in James's band?

5. Shorty compared the music in New Orleans to gumbo. What is gumbo? How did the music of the Mardi Gras resemble gumbo?

6. What was Shorty's first trombone like?

7. How did Shorty learn to play the trombone?

8. What was the New Orleans Jazz and Heritage Festival? How did Shorty get recognized at this event? How did he get to the stage?

9. Was Trombone Shorty ever able to join his brother's band?

10. What is the name of Trombone Shorty's band now? How is Trombone Shorty like his brother in working with the new band participants?

11. Who is Bo Diddley and what is his connection to Shorty?

12. Read the author's note at the end of the story. What types of things did you learn about Shorty?

Select related children's literature

Orgill, Roxanne. *If I Only Had a Horn.* Boston: Houghton Mifflin Harcourt, 1997.

Pinkney, Andrea Davis. *Duke Ellington.* New York: Hyperion, 1998.

Russell-Brown, Katheryn. *Little Melba and Her Big Trombone.* New York: Lee and Low, 2014.

Weatherford, Carole Boston. *Before John Was a Jazz Giant.* New York: Henry Holt and Company, 2008.

Crown: An Ode To The Fresh Cut

by Derrick Barnes
and Gordon C. James   Grades 2–5

Summary

As stated by Derrick Barnes in "A Note from the Author," this book focuses on "the beautiful, raw, smart, perceptive, assured humanity of black boys/sons/brothers/nephews/grandsons, and how they see themselves when they highly approve of their reflections in the mirror."

Barnes, Derrick and James, Gordon C. *Crown: An Ode to the Fresh Cut*. Chicago: Bolden, 2017.

Questions for discussion, written responses, and/or research

1. Summarize the story in your own words.

2. What is the author's purpose in writing this book?

3. What does the author state are some of the positive things that could happen to a young man resulting from a fresh cut?

4. There are other gentlemen in the shop also getting a fresh cut. The young man predicts what their individual professions may be. On which characteristics does he base his predictions?

5. How do the illustrations in the book support the key message of the story?

6. What does it mean when the young man says "He looks that FRESH!" (page 13) about one of the patrons who has just had a fresh cut?

7. How does the young man feel after he got his fresh cut?

8. How does he imagine the other people in the shop will react?

9. How will you perform on your next English test? What is the reason?

10. What will your mom say? Why is this so important?

11. Why is it important to tip the barber? What does a tip show to the barber?

12. This book is a feel-good book. List some ways the young man who just received the fresh cut feels good.

Select related children's literature

Barnes, Derrick and James, Gordon C. *I Am Every Good Thing.* New York: Penguin Random House, 2020.

I Am Every Good Thing

**by Derrick Barnes
and Gordon C. James**   Grades 2–5

OF NOTE: This book is dedicated to a number of African-American young men who were victims of fatal shootings, including Tamir Rice, Trayvon Martin, Michael Brown, E.J. Bradford, Jordan Edwards, Jordan Davis, and Julian Mallory.

Summary

A beautifully illustrated and well-written story focusing on a child's self-esteem. A celebration of the confident child.

Barnes, Derrick and James, Gordon C. *I Am Every Good Thing*. New York: Penguin Random House, 2020.

Questions for discussion, written responses, and/or research

1. Summarize the book in your own words.

2. What do you think the author's purpose is in writing this book?

3. How do the illustrations support the story?

4. The young man who is narrating the story has big hopes and dreams. What are they?

5. The story is very inspirational and uplifting. Select some passages from the book that demonstrate these qualities.

6. What is meant by the phrase on page 23: "Although I am something like a superhero, every now and then I am afraid. I am not what they might call me and I will not answer to any name that is not my own. I am what I say I am"?

7. What is the young man afraid of? What are some things he will do to deal with his fear?

8. On the last page of the book the young man says, "I am worthy to be loved" (page 29). Having read the story, why is this an appropriate ending?

Select related children's literature

Barnes, Derrick and James, Gordon C. *Crown: An Ode to the Fresh Cut*. Chicago: Bolden, 2017.

I Believe I Can

by Grace Byers   **Grades K–3**

Summary

There is no end to the possibilities that can be achieved by the young girls and boys in this delightful poem. A feel-good book to be enjoyed and to serve as a discussion for all students.

Byers, Grace. *I Believe I Can*. New York: Balzer and Bray, 2020.

Questions for discussion, written responses, and/or research

1. The narrators of this story are the children pictured in the illustrations. Each of them believes they can accomplish many things. What are some things you have accomplished?

2. One child states that "like the oceans, she runs deep" (page 2). What do you think she means by this?

3. What does a "lion's roar" depict? Which human characteristics come to mind when you hear this phrase?

4. "I am worthy because I'm me and there is value to my name" (pages 9–10). What does this line from the book mean to you?

5. One child compares himself first to the soil and then to the sky. Discuss these two comparisons and what they mean to you.

6. What is the overall message in this poem?

7. How do mistakes contribute to a person's growth in good ways?

8. What does the book recommend we do when we don't succeed at something?

9. The illustration on the page where the poem states, "I know I can do anything" (page 28) shows six children. What do you notice about them?

10. The same illustration is on the back cover of the book. Why is this such an important illustration?

Select related children's literature

Barnes, Derrick and James, Gordon C. *I Am Every Good Thing*. New York: Penguin Random House, 2020.

Beaumont, Karen. *I Like Myself!* Boston: Houghton Mifflin Harcourt, 2006.

Curcio, Anthony. *The Boy Who Never Gave Up: Stephen Curry*. www.sportivabooks.com, 2018.

Domoney, Cathy. *The Magic Is Inside You*. North Charleston, SC: Cathy Domoney, 2011.

Gaines, Joanna. *The World Needs Who You Were Made to Be.* Nashville: Tommy Nelson, 2020.

Johnson, Angela. *A Girl Like Me.* Minneapolis: Millbrook Press, 2004.

Killiebrew, J. *There Is a Girl Headed to the White House.* n.p., U.S.: Dr. Jazz Killiebrew, Ph.D., 2020.

Firebird

by Misty Copeland   Grades K–3

Summary

A young dancer, who aspires to be like Misty Copeland, is unsure of her goal. She lacks confidence and feels she could not accomplish some of the beautiful and difficult moves of a dancer like Misty. Misty assures her that ballerinas all start out this way and through hard work and practice she can become just like her. Beautiful illustrations embellish this story of a young dancer who achieves her dream.

Copeland, Misty. *Firebird*. New York: G.P. Putnam, 2014.

Questions for discussion, written responses, and/or research

1. The author of this book is Misty Copeland. Who is Misty Copeland? Do some research to find out.

2. Have you ever been to a ballet? What is it like?

3. Have you ever taken ballet lessons? How did you feel the first time you danced?

4. Looking at the story and the illustrations, why is this book entitled *Firebird*?

5. The young dancer feels like she will not be able to become a great ballet dancer. What are Misty's words of encouragement to her?

6. Look up the word *arabesque*. How is this word used in the story? What does this word mean in the context of dancing?

7. In the story, Misty says that she and the dancer will "pirouette tightly as the curls on our head" (page 25). What does this mean?

8. There are many comparisons used in the story to help describe what ballet is like. These comparisons are called metaphors. An example from the story is "you will soar, become a swan, a beauty, a firebird for sure" (page 21). What does this metaphor mean in terms of ballet? What are some other metaphors in the story and what do they mean in the context of ballet?

The Boy Who Became King

by Anthony Curcio   Grades 1–4

Summary

LeBron James, NBA superstar, has been playing professional basketball since 2003 and still plays today. Born in Akron, Ohio, in 1984, he was raised by his mother, his grandmother, and his great-grandmother. After his grandmother and great-grandmother passed away, he was raised by his mother. They moved many times while she looked for work. LeBron originally started out as a young football player who quickly became great at football, but his true love was basketball and in fourth grade he signed up to play with a kids' basketball team supervised by an amazing adult coach. The rest is history. He went on to become one of the greatest basketball players of all time.

Curcio, Anthony. *The Boy Who Became King: LeBron James.* Columbia, SC: Anthony Curcio, 2021.

Questions for discussion, written responses, and/or research

1. Why did LeBron miss a lot of school at a young age?

2. How was he different from the other kids of his age?

3. When LeBron finally went to school, why was it so hard for him?

4. When he started to play football, why was he an immediate star?

5. When asked to join the fourth-grade basketball team, how did LeBron become such a great player?

6. LeBron dreamed that he would someday play for the NBA. What is the NBA and for what teams did he eventually play?

7. His basketball coach and his wife, Frankie and Pam Walker, offered to have LeBron live with them when his mother had to move again looking for work. How did LeBron's life change living with the Walkers?

8. LeBron was going to school regularly when he lived with the Walkers. How did he do in school? Why was he much more successful in school this time than he had been in the past?

9. LeBron was a great player at a young age. How did the general public find out about him?

10. Why did LeBron decide not to go to college?

11. While "King James," as he is called, is a legend, what about his personal life distinguishes him as a true role model?

12. Who is LeBron's favorite fan? How is she a part of all the people-helping projects he has done?

Select related children's literature

Curcio, Anthony. *The Boy Who Never Gave Up: Stephen Curry.* www.sportivabooks.com, 2018.

Feiner, Beck. *Basketball Legends Alphabet.* n.p., U.S.: Alphabet Legends Pty Ltd., 2019.

James, LeBron. *I Promise.* New York: HarperCollins, 2020.

Rich, Francine Poppo. *Larry Bird.* West Bay Shore, NY: Blue Martin, 2009.

Parker Looks Up

by Parker Curry and Jessica Curry   Grades K–4

Summary

Parker Curry, her mother, and her sister decided to take a trip to the museum on a rainy day and chose the Donald W. Reynolds Center for American Art and Portraiture in Washington, D.C. Along with their friend, Gia, they toured the museum looking at all the paintings, and what they saw is described in beautiful detail and illustrations throughout this book. Parker loved to dance and saw paintings of stunning ballerinas, but it was the last portrait that mesmerized her. She saw much more than the portrait. She saw the endless possibilities it inspired.

Curry, Parker and Curry, Jessica. *Parker Looks Up*. New York: Simon and Schuster, 2019.

Questions for discussion, written responses, and/or research

1. Where do you think Parker and her family live? Give reasons for your answer.

2. What is the National Portrait Gallery in Washington, D.C.?

3. Whose portraits do you think may be on display there? Do some research to see how your predictions relate to the actual portraits displayed.

4. What were some of the portraits the girls saw?

5. Name something fascinating about the portrait "Blooming Flowers", depicted in the book.

6. Do you recognize any of the people whose portraits appear in the story? Who do you think they are?

7. Why was Parker so excited to see a portrait of ballerinas?

8. What did Parker see when "Parker looked up"? Who is this famous lady?

9. There are many words used to describe this person – mother, lawyer, courageous, smart, caring, dynamic, advocate, inspirational, hero. Why are these words so fitting?

10. Near the end of the book, the writer states, "In that moment, Parker saw more than just a portrait – she saw a road before her with endless possibilities" (page 25). What do you think this means?

A Place Inside Of Me

by Zetta Elliot   Grades K–5

Summary

Through a beautiful, convincing poem, the author successfully describes the collage of emotions a black child experiences as he confronts the different times in a year of his life.

Elliot, Zetta. *A Place Inside of Me.* New York: Farrar, Straus and Giroux, 2020.

Questions for discussion, written responses, and/or research

1. The young man who is narrating the poem talks about a place deep inside of him. What do you think he means?

2. Which words in the poem describe these feelings inside of him?

3. How does he describe the emotion of joy? When does this emotion appear? Which words does the author use to describe this emotion? When you feel joy, what does that feel like? When does joy happen?

4. How does he describe the emotion of sorrow? When does this emotion appear? What are some events that cause sorrow?

5. How does he describe fear? When does fear happen?

6. When the young man speaks of anger, which words does he use to describe it? How do you feel when you are angry? Use the illustrations in the story to explain which events evoke anger in this young man.

7. When he speaks of hunger, is he speaking about food? What is the young man hungry for?

8. Who are some of the famous African-American people whose photos appear in the book?

9. The theme of this book is uplifting. What do you think the theme is and what makes it uplifting?

Ambitious Girl

by Meena Harris   Grades K–4

Summary

Meena is the niece of Kamala Harris, who was elected vice president of the United States in 2021. The book is dedicated to her grandmother, Kamala's mother, for the inspiration and encouragement to be anything she aspires to be. The little girl who narrates the story has the ambition to be who she aspires to be with confidence, purpose and power. She attributes her ambition to not only her grandmother, but to the women who came before her. This is an uplifting book with the message anything is possible if you work at it.

Harris, Meena. *Ambitious Girl.* New York: Little, Brown and Company Books for Young Readers, 2021.

Questions for discussion, written responses, and/or research

1. According to the girl telling the story, what is ambition?

2. Do you think Meena is telling the story? Explain your answer.

3. The book starts off by saying, "Don't let anyone tell you who you are. You tell them who you are" (page 6). What is meant by this opening?

4. What does Grandma mean when she says, "You may be the first someday, but don't be the last – make space for more" (page 17)?

5. What does the expression "opening doors" used in the story mean to you?

6. How does the girl telling the story define these important words: "Persistent…Assertive… Confident…Proud"? Why do you think these are important words as you work to accomplish your goals?

7. What does an ambitious girl do if she fails at something? Why do you think this is important?

8. What does the expression, "I am more than ready to use my voice" (page 24) mean to you?

9. At the end of the story, the author's note contains Meena's purpose in writing the book. What was her purpose?

Select related children's literature

Byers, Grace. *I Believe I Can*. New York: Balzer and Bray, 2020.

Kamala And Maya's Big Idea

by Meena Harris   Grades K–5

Summary

Kamala and Maya are sisters. As young children, they had the idea of making their empty apartment court-yard into a playground. This book, based on a true story, focuses on making a difference in a community despite having obstacles to overcome.

Harris, Meena. *Kamala and Maya's Big Idea*. New York: HarperCollins, 2020.

Questions for discussion, written responses, and/or research

1. What was Kamala and Maya's big idea for the apartment building's courtyard?

2. Do you think it was a good idea? Why?

3. Kamala and Maya's mother suggested the sisters write a letter to the landlord. What is a landlord?

4. What do you think Kamala and Maya should say in the letter to the landlord? How many of your ideas are actually included in their letter?

5. The word "maybe" becomes an important word throughout the story. Why? Illustrate your answer with some examples from the text.

6. Were you ever told "maybe" by a parent in response to something you wanted? Did the "maybe" become a yes or no, and why?

7. In the story, there are the following statements: "No one can do everything. But everyone can do something" (page 19). Find examples in the story that show these statements are true.

8. What were some of the obstacles Kamala, Maya, and the apartment community had to overcome to be successful with the project?

9. The community needed to raise money for one more piece of equipment to complete the project. What piece of equipment did they need? Name some of their ideas to raise money. What else could they have done to raise money for this project?

10. "Hooray for the 'per-sisters!'" (page 26) What made Kamala and Maya per-sisters?

11. What have you learned from the story?

12. Have you ever encountered a situation where you were determined to be successful? What obstacles did you have to overcome to reach your goal? How did you overcome each one?

Select related children's literature

Harris, Kamala. *Superheroes Are Everywhere.* New York: Philomel Books, 2019.

Harris, Meena. *Ambitious Girl.* New York: Little, Brown and Company Books for Young Readers, 2021.

She's Got This

by Laurie Hernandez   Grades K–3

Summary

Zoe, an aspiring gymnast, is excited about gymnastics until her first fall. Then she doesn't want to go back. With the encouragement and support of her family, she does return to the gym – and flies!

Hernandez, Laurie. *She's Got This*. New York: HarperCollins, 2018.

Questions for discussion, written responses, and/or research

1. What is a gymnast? List some of the things a gymnast does.

2. Do you know a gymnast? What special skills do they have?

3. How did Zoe become interested in gymnastics? How did her parents help support her dream to become a gymnast?

4. When Zoe first tried the balance beam, she fell off. How did she hurt herself? There is a line in the story that states, "her heart hurts, too" (page 10). What do you think that means?

5. Did you ever have your heart hurt like Zoe? What were the circumstances? What made you feel better?

6. How did Zoe's family react when Zoe didn't want to go back to the gym? What important lesson were they trying to teach her?

7. When Zoe did go back to the gym, how had her attitude changed?

8. This story is written by Laurie Hernandez, an American gymnast who won Olympic gold. Research her life and write about her accomplishments. How similar to Zoe's life is Laurie's?

Select related children's literature

Burk, Rachelle. *The Story of Simone Biles.* Emeryville, CA: Rockledge Press, 2020.

Fishman, Jon. *Gabby Douglas.* Minneapolis: Lerner, 2013.

Morgan, Sally J. *Simone Biles: Golden Girl of Gymnastics.* New York: Penguin Random House, 2020.

Kids Who Are Changing The World

by Sheila Sweeny Higginson   Grades K–4

Summary

This book contains interesting short biographies about children who are changing the world. Among others whose work on societal problems has made a positive impact, you will meet Jahkil Naeem Jackson, Natalie Hampton, Gitanjali Rao, and Joris Hutchinson. The book is part of a series entitled *Learning to Read*.

Higginson, Sheila Sweeny. *Kids Who Are Changing the World*. New York: Simon Spotlight, 2019.

Questions for discussion, written responses, and/or research

1. The book is divided into four chapters, each about a child who has solved a major societal problem with impressive results. Read one story a day and discuss each child's accomplishments.

2. The book provides valuable information about children who were diverse achievers. Explore the brief summaries at the end which outline the accomplishments of two other children.

Salt In His Shoes

by Deloris Jordan
and Roslyn M. Jordan   Grades 2–5

Summary

Michael Jordan, an NBA basketball superstar in the late twentieth and early twenty-first centuries, was not one of the tallest kids growing up. Taunted about his height when he was younger by one of the players on the opposing team of his Saturday basketball games, Michael turned to his mother for advice. She told him that if he put salt in his shoes and said his prayers each night, he would grow. While he didn't grow in the next four months, he followed his father's advice to play with determination, practice, and giving it his all.

Jordan, Deloris and Jordan, Roslyn M. *Salt in His Shoes.* New York: Aladdin, 2000.

Questions for discussion, written responses, and/or research

1. Michael Jordan became one of the greatest NBA basketball players of all time. How tall was he when he played as a pro? Research the heights of other NBA superstars.

2. This book was written by Michael Jordan's mother and sister. How many siblings did Michael have?

3. How did Michael feel about going to the park with his brothers on Saturdays to play basketball against another team?

4. What advice did Michael's father give him to encourage him to play?

5. Michael was a victim of bullying by an opposing team member. How did he handle this? How did he eventually deal with the bully?

6. Why is bullying such a bad thing? What should we do if we are ever confronted by a bully?

What Will I Be?

by Jayla Joseph   Grades 3–6

Summary

Displaying the words, "There are no limits on the greatness we can achieve" on its front cover and last page, this book inspires us to be the best we can be. It tells us about different professions and what each one involves.

Joseph, Jayla. *What Will I Be?* Coppell, TX: Independently Published, 2020.

Questions for discussion, written responses, and/or research

1. Have you ever thought about what you want to be or do when you grow up? Share your answers.

2. Discuss what skills are needed for your chosen profession and think about how you can learn these skills.

3. What does an oceanographer do? Which skills do you think an oceanographer would need?

4. The airline pilot has an exciting job. Have you ever been on an airplane? Where did you fly to? Use

Google to find out in which states or countries each destination is located.

5. What other professions are discussed in the book? Do any of them interest you? Why?

6. Suppose you want to be a writer. Name some writers you have heard of or whose works you have read. What type of stories would you be interested in writing?

7. What are some high-tech jobs you could do? Which skills do you think are involved in each job?

8. Being a lawyer is also an interesting profession. What do lawyers do? How do you become a lawyer?

9. Make a list of the things you think the following professions involve:

- Entrepreneur

- Doctor

- Teacher

- Firefighter

- Law enforcement officer

There Is A Girl Headed To The White House

by J. Killiebrew   Grades 2–6

Summary

An uplifting and inspirational book about a girl who can be anything she wants to be, even the first lady of the United States. It is also a topical book, with the election in 2020 of Kamala Harris, the first African-American South Asian female vice president of the United States.

Killiebrew, J. *There Is a Girl Headed to the White House.* n.p., U.S.: Dr. Jazz Killiebrew, Ph.D., 2020.

Questions for discussion, written responses, and/or research

1. "Not everyone can be famous but everyone can be great" (page 5). What do you think the author means by this statement?

2. Why does the author suggest we should always do our best?

3. Considering recent events in society, why do you think there have been protests with people carrying signs like "No Justice, No Peace"?

4. What does the author mean when she states, "The World belongs to those who believe. I Can and I Will" (page 11)?

5. What does "own every room you enter" (page 12) mean to you?

6. How can your interactions with other people help you be "anything you want to be"?

7. In what ways is our mind our most valuable asset?

8. Summarize the story. What is its message?

Select related children's literature

Harris, Meena. *Ambitious Girl.* New York: Little, Brown and Company Books for Young Readers, 2021.

Gary And The Great Inventors

by Akura Marshall   Grades K–3

Summary

Each Sunday, Gary and his twin brother, Isaac, go on a trip to Mr. Baker's Laundromat in Washington, D.C. with their parents. When they arrive, they see a sign, "Organic Dry Cleaning Now Available". The twins have questions for Mr. Baker about the dry-cleaning machine so he gives them the history and shows them where to find other answers to their questions.

Marshall, Akura. *Gary and the Great Inventors.* n.p., U.S.: Our Children's Network, Inc., 2018.

Questions for discussion, written responses, and/or research

1. Why did the kids like going to Mr. Baker's Laundromat?

2. What and where is Washington, D.C.?

3. How can you tell from the story that the twins' friend didn't make the trip with them to the laundromat?

4. Gary has a question for Mr. Baker based on the sign in the window. What is the question? How does Mr. Baker respond?

5. How is the dry-cleaning machine different from a regular washing machine?

6. Do you ever go to the dry cleaner with a family member? What kinds of clothes do you bring?

7. What do you think a patent is? Why was it unusual for the inventor of the dry-cleaning machine to get a patent when he did?

8. How is Gary inspired by his visit to Mr. Baker? What does he tell his family on the way home?

Select related children's literature

Jones, Lynda. *Five Brilliant Scientists*. New York: Scholastic, 2000.

McLaurin, Patrice. *Have You Thanked an Inventor Today?* Lawrenceville, GA: Khemrah Publishing, 2016.

The Undefeated, ESPN. *The Fierce 44: Black Americans Who Shook Up the World*. Boston: Houghton Mifflin Harcourt, 2019.

A Boy Like You

by Frank Murphy   Grades 3–6

Summary

The book opens with the line, "There are billions and billions and billions of people in the world. But you are the only YOU there is" and goes on to talk about all the wonderful ways you can be a boy. A great book for building confidence and self-esteem, it showcases diversity beautifully.

Murphy, Frank. *A Boy Like You*. Ann Arbor, MI: Sleeping Bear Press, 2019.

Questions for discussion, written responses, and/or research

1. This book carries an uplifting message: each of us is unique. What are some of the ways each of you is unique? How does this contribute to cultural and racial diversity?

2. Why does the world need each of us?

3. The boy in the story is curious about math problems and science experiments. What are some of the everyday things you are curious about?

4. How does the author explain that fear and bravery can be partners, when they appear to be so opposite in meaning?

5. Why does the author suggest boys ask lots of questions when they are in school?

6. Why should boys dream big?

7. Why is it important to listen to the stories of other people?

8. How do the illustrations in the book depict diverse cultures and races?

9. Why does the author suggest that we leave every person "better than you found them"?

10. What does the author mean when he says, "You are original"? What are some of the ways you are original?

A Girl Like You

by Frank Murphy
and Carla Murphy   Grades 3–6

Summary

The book starts off in the same way as *A Boy Like You* – there is only one YOU – and goes on to describe all the wonderful ways you can be a girl. It is a great confidence and self-esteem builder for girls, and showcases racial and cultural diversity throughout.

Murphy, Frank and Murphy, Carla. *A Girl Like You*. Ann Arbor, MI: Sleeping Bear Press, 2020.

Questions for discussion, written responses, and/or research

1. How can a girl can be brave? Use the story and illustrations to help you answer this question.

2. What are some of your dreams? How do you think you can make them happen?

3. What do the authors mean when they say a girl should be bold? They use pairs of antonyms to compare boldness in different settings. How can a girl be bold if she is quiet and if she is loud? Young or old? Tall or small?

4. When is the right time to say you are sorry?

5. "Thoughtful girls have empathy" (page 14). What does this mean? Can you think of a situation in which you were empathetic to someone?

6. The story tells all girls (and boys, too) to "embrace the body they are in" (page 17). How do you interpret this statement?

7. Girls should have different hairstyles. How are your hair and clothes an expression of yourself? When do you change your hairstyle?

8. How is cultural and racial diversity shown throughout the book?

9. How are disabilities presented in the book? Why is it important to treat people with disabilities as normally as possible?

10. Look at the writing activity at the end of the book. Have a discussion with your class or parents about the great questions listed there.

Little Melba And Her Big Trombone

by Katheryn Russell-Brown   Grades 3–6

Summary

Melba Doretta Liston was an African-American trombone player, songwriter, and arranger. Melba grew up with music. She dreamed about music. Music was her life. She started playing the trombone at age seven and continued to play throughout her life. When she started playing, the trombone was considerably bigger than she was. With support from her family, she taught herself to play and learned how to maneuver her body so she could stretch the slide of the trombone. She faced challenges when she moved with her mother to Los Angeles from Kansas City in 1937. She traveled with Billie Holiday and encountered racism in the South, but she triumphed in the face of this and became an international star.

Russell-Brown, Katheryn. *Little Melba and Her Big Trombone.* New York: Lee and Low, 2014.

Questions for discussion, written responses, and/or research

1. When and where was Melba born?

2. What type of music did Melba love as a child?

3. Melba received a player piano as a child. What is a player piano?

4. At what age did Melba start playing the trombone? What were some of the problems she encountered playing this instrument?

5. Why did Melba and her mother move to Los Angeles in 1937?

6. What kind of student was she in her new school? What did the principal decide to do as a result of her test scores?

7. Why were other students jealous of her? How did Melba handle this?

8. Melba began traveling the country with a band when she was just seventeen. Name some of the cities she and the band visited to perform.

9. Who was Billie Holiday? What difficulties did Melba and Billie encounter when they traveled to the South to perform? What was Melba's reaction?

10. Which famous jazz performers wanted to play Melba's original music?

11. Melba began traveling internationally to play her music. List some of the places she traveled to.

12. Read the afterword at the end of the story, which details more about the life of Melba Liston. Which facts do you find interesting?

Select related children's literature

Andrews, Troy. *Trombone Shorty*. New York: Abrams, 2015.

Black Boy, Black Boy

by Crown Shepherd   Grades K–6

Summary

This book, which is excellent for reading aloud to any group of children, promotes self-esteem for young black boys. It encourages readers to believe there is nothing that can't be accomplished if you dream it and have hopes and aspirations, and helps build confidence in their ability to accomplish goals.

Shepherd, Crown. *Black Boy, Black Boy.* St. Paul, MN: Beaver's Pond Press, 2020.

Questions for discussion, written responses, and/or research

1. The story is inspirational. What does this mean?

2. What do you want to be when you grow up? What would you have to learn to be successful in achieving this?

3. Many different professions are discussed in the book and each one is accompanied by a beautiful illustration. Name some of these professions. How does each picture illustrate the profession?

4. What is the author's purpose in writing this book?

5. What is creativity? Can you think of some times/ events where you have been creative?

6. Look at the last two-page illustration in the book. Why do you think both boys and girls are shown?

Select related children's literature

Barnes, Derrick and James, Gordon C. *I Am Every Good Thing.* New York: Penguin Random House, 2020.

Domoney, Cathy. *The Magic Is Inside You.* North Charleston, SC: Cathy Domoney, 2011.

Rodriguez, Ayesha. *I Am... Positive Affirmations for Brown Boys.* www.ayesharodriguez.com, 2016.

Talbert, Lyn-Sisson and Talbert, David E. *The Square Root of Possible.* New York: Penguin Random House, 2020.

Big Hair, Don't Care

by Crystal Swain-Bates   Grades K–3

Summary

The little girl in the story has big hair. In this beautiful rhyming poem, she describes all the styles she can make with her hair and even though her hair is big enough to block out someone's view in a movie theater, she doesn't care. Instead, she gently warns people not to sit directly in back of her at the movies. The story is uplifting and the illustrations support the poem. Perfect for young children.

Swain-Bates, Crystal. *Big Hair, Don't Care*. Walnut, CA: Goldest Karat Publishing, 2013.

Questions for discussion, written responses, and/or research

1. Why does the girl in the story not care that she has big hair?

2. Why does she tell the reader not to sit behind her and her friend at the movies?

3. Why does she sometimes lose at hide-and-seek?

4. What are some of the hairstyles she can get designed for her hair?

5. As you read through the poem, pick out some of the pairs of rhyming words.

6. Why can you find her in a crowd of people?

7. What did you learn from the story?

Select related children's literature

Barnes, Derrick and James, Gordon C. *Crown: An Ode to the Fresh Cut*. Chicago: Bolden, 2017.

Tarpley, Natasha Anastasia. *I Love My Hair*. New York: Little, Brown and Company Books for Young Readers, 1998.

Harlem's Little Blackbird

by Renee Watson   Grades 2–6

Summary

Florence Mills, born in Washington, D.C. in 1896 as the daughter of slaves, was known as Harlem's Little Blackbird. Learning to sing spiritual music from her mother, Florence sang and danced for everyone. As word about her talent circulated, she was invited to perform at one of Washington's theaters. When she arrived with her friends, all of whom were Negro, none of them was allowed into the whites-only theater, even though Florence was performing. Florence refused to perform unless her friends were admitted so the manager "snuck" them in. When she and her family moved to New York, Florence and her sisters became known for their singing and dancing. The Mills Sisters performed in New York, but Florence always stood out. She became a big part of the Harlem Renaissance.

Watson, Renee. *Harlem's Little Blackbird.* New York: Penguin Random House, 2012.

Questions for discussion, written response and/or research

1. Florence was the daughter of former slaves. What special talent did she have?

2. What was the cakewalk?

3. What kind of student was Florence? Why?

4. Florence was asked to perform at a theater in Washington. What happened when she and her friends arrived? What was Florence's reaction? How did the issue get resolved?

5. How did Florence use her voice to get a positive outcome at the theater?

6. Florence earned a role in a Broadway play called *Shuffle Along*. What was the purpose of this show?

7. What was the Harlem Renaissance? You may have to use Google to find out. Name some of the famous people of the Harlem Renaissance.

8. What happened when Florence traveled overseas to perform? How did Florence deal with this issue?

9. Who was Mr. Ziegfeld? What offer did he make Florence? What was her response? Why?

10. How did Florence promote equal rights for black people?

11. When she was invited back to London to perform, what reception did she receive?

12. Florence disguised herself in London so she could do good things for the people. What types of things did she do?

13. Florence died of illness at a young age. Thousands of people came to her funeral. Name some of the people who came to pay their respects.

14. In the author's note at the end of the book, we learn that Florence's voice was never recorded. How did she become so famous?

Select related children's literature

Ringgold, Faith. *Harlem Renaissance Party*. New York: Amistad, 2015.

The Other Side

by Jacqueline Woodson   Grades 2–5

Summary

Clover, who is black, and Annie, who is white, lived in a town where a fence separated black people from white people. On many days Clover would see Annie sitting on the fence. One day, Clover went over to the fence and the girls introduced themselves and struck up a conversation. Both girls figured out they should not cross the fence, but as neither was told they couldn't sit on it, they did. Soon four of Clover's friends joined them on the fence. The girls' wish was that someone, someday would knock down that fence. The illustrations are beautifully supportive of the story.

Woodson, Jacqueline. *The Other Side.* New York: Nancy Paulson, 2001.

Questions for discussion, written responses, and/or research

1. What is the theme of the story?

2. Why did Clover's mother say it wasn't safe to play on the other side of the fence?

3. Annie sat on the fence each day alone. Why do you think other girls didn't sit with her?

4. When Annie asked Clover and her friends if she could join them in jumping rope, one of Clover's friends said no. Why do you think this was? What do you think Clover would have said?

5. What was Mama's answer to Clover's question about why the black people were separated from the white people?

6. Why do you think Annie always played near the fence on the white side?

7. Under which circumstances did the girls finally meet?

8. Clover and Annie knew each couldn't cross the fence, but they saw nothing wrong with sitting on it. Why did they do this?

9. Initially, Clover's friends didn't seem to like that Clover sat on the fence with Annie. What happened that got all the girls on the fence?

10. What did you learn from this story?

Select related children's literature

Memory, Jelani. *A Kids Book About Racism.* Portland, OR: A Kids Book About, Inc., 2019.

PART SIX
DIVERSITY IN HISTORY

What Color Is My World?

by Kareem Abdul-Jabbar
and Raymond Obstfeld   Grades 1–5

Summary

This book is the story of two children who are moving with their parents into an old home that needs to be refurbished by Mr. Mital, the handyman. The children are asked by their mother to sweep up, which they don't do as well as they should because they become engrossed in Mr. Mital's stories. He tells them about sixteen unknown African-American inventors, all of whom invented or laid the foundation for the invention of many things we use today, but who didn't receive credit for their work. The vignettes of each inventor are brief but informative and could be read throughout Black History Month.

Abdul-Jabbar, Kareem and Obstfeld, Raymond. *What Color Is My World? The Lost History of African-American Inventors*. Somerville, MA: Candlewick Press, 2012.

Questions for discussion, written responses, and/or research

1. The book is divided into six chapters which tell the story of a handyman who introduced the lives of unknown black inventors to the children, Ella and Herbie. Read one chapter, then on each of the next three days read one of the vignettes it contains and discuss them with your class to learn about what the authors name "the lost history of African-American inventors" (inside cover page).

Select related children's literature

Adero, Malika. *A Black Woman Did That.* New York: Downtown Bookworks, 2019.

Asim, Jabari. *A Child's Introduction to African American History.* New York: Black Dog and Leventhal Publishers, 2018.

Beckner, Chrisanne. *100 African Americans Who Shaped American History.* San Mateo, CA: Bluewood Books, 1995.

Harrison, Vashti. *Little Leaders: Bold Women in Black History.* New York: Little, Brown and Company Books for Young Readers, 2017.

A Child's Introduction To African American History

by Jabari Asim   Grades K–8

Summary

With a focus on how the African-American experience helped to shape America, this book offers many learning opportunities. It provides an exemplary timeline of African-American history through words, illustration, vignettes, and a fold-out timeline, all of which can be used by teachers, parents, and children throughout the year in the study of black history and during Black History Month in February.

Asim, Jabari. *A Child's Introduction to African American History.* New York: Black Dog and Leventhal Publishers, 2018.

Questions for discussion, written responses, and/or research

There are numerous ways to use this resource. Here are some suggestions.

1. Display the fold-out timeline at the back of the book in your room, or ask if you can put it up in your classroom.

2. During Black History Month, read vignettes about African Americans in the book.

3. Read and discuss the section on black history.

4. Research one of the political trailblazers and prepare a brief report to orally present to your class.

5. What was the Harlem Renaissance? Who were some of the famous artists and entertainers who were part of the Renaissance?

6. What does the phrase "separate but equal" mean? What did it apply to?

7. Who was the first African-American female millionaire in the United States? How did she make her money and what are some of the philanthropic things she did with it?

8. What is the NAACP? When was it formed? Who were some African Americans who started this organization?

9. What was the case Brown vs. Board of Education? What was the outcome of this case?

10. Come up with some suggestions of your own for using this book.

Memphis, Martin And The Mountaintop

by Alice Faye Duncan   Grades 4–8

Summary

This book tells the story of the Memphis Sanitation Strike of 1968, when sanitation workers fought for better wages and working conditions. The mayor would not agree to a pay increase from the $1.70 per hour the workers were being paid. The strike lasted several months. Dr. Martin Luther King, Jr. came to Memphis to give support to a massive march he planned in the spring. When he returned to Memphis after the march, the protest turned into a riot. Dr. King had wanted to organize a more peaceful march, and he gave a famous speech telling the people they would get to the mountaintop but it may be without him. On April 4, 1968, Dr. King was assassinated by an escaped convict, James Earl Ray. On April 8, the peaceful march took place, led by his widow, Coretta Scott King, and the Southern Leadership Conference, helping to end the Memphis Sanitation Strike.

Duncan, Alice Faye. *Memphis, Martin and the Mountaintop.* New York: Calkins Creek, 2018.

Questions for discussion, written responses, and/or research

1. Roughly how long did the sanitation strike in Memphis last?

2. What had happened in the early part of February to two sanitation workers? Why did this happen?

3. Lorraine, the child in the story, marched with adults for better pay and safer working conditions for the sanitation workers. She states that her father marched for her. What did she mean by this statement?

4. What were some of the organizations that wanted to help the marchers? In what ways could they help?

5. Why did Lorraine's father not quit the strike and return to work?

6. Who was Dr. Martin Luther King, Jr.? How did he get involved in the sanitation strike? What type of protest did he encourage the marchers to conduct?

7. What was the Civil Rights Act of 1964? Who was the president at that time?

8. How did Lorraine's parents get the news each day? Why did they get it this way?

9. What is meant by the term "silver rights"?

10. Why did Martin Luther King, Jr. cancel the initial peaceful protest march planned for the month of March?

11. What were some of Dr. Martin Luther King, Jr.'s goals for the working poor?

12. What happened to make Mama say, "Sometimes bad people mess things up for the good people doing good" (page 19)?

13. How did the sanitation strike finally end? What were the positive outcomes for the sanitation workers?

Select related children's literature

Pinkney, Andrea Davis and Pinkney, Brian. *Martin and Mahalia: His Words, Her Song.* New York: Little, Brown and Company Books for Young Readers, 2013.

The Youngest Marcher: The Story Of Audrey Faye Hendricks, A Young Civil Rights Activist

by Cynthia Levinson   Grades 3–8

Summary

An amazing and true story about the youngest civil rights activist, Audrey Faye Hendricks, who was only nine when she began participating in the civil rights movement. A young advocate for the abolishment of segregation laws in Birmingham, Alabama, and a bold and confident figure, Audrey took part in civil rights marches, which got her arrested and sent to jail.

Levinson, Cynthia. *The Youngest Marcher: The Story of Audrey Faye Hendricks, a Young Civil Rights Activist.* New York: Atheneum Books for Young Readers, 2017.

Questions for discussion, written responses, and/or research

1. The story opens with dinner at the family table with special guests, including Mike. Who was Mike?

2. At nine years old, Audrey knew about racial bias and segregation. Give some examples of racial bias she experienced or was aware of.

3. What types of advice did Martin Luther King give the congregants of the church he preached at?

4. Why did Martin Luther King suggest the people peacefully protest until they get arrested?

5. Why did Audrey decide to volunteer to go to jail?

6. Audrey was the youngest of the children in the peaceful protest and the only student from her school. Despite the fact that she knew no one, she was determined to get arrested. Why?

7. How long was Audrey's jail sentence? Describe some of her experiences while she was there.

8. One day she was taken to a room where she was questioned by four white men. What did they want to know about Audrey?

9. Audrey was unhappy in jail, but she had a goal. What was the goal and why? Did she reach it?

10. What good outcomes did Audrey see as she watched TV?

11. What did Birmingham do about their segregation laws? List some of the positive results that came from this.

12. In 2008, Audrey Faye Hendricks said, "What a difference the children's march has made in this nation" (page 33). What did she mean by this quote?

Select related children's literature

Allen, Tessa. *Sometimes People March.* New York: Balzer and Bray, 2020.

Robinson, Monica Clark. *Let the Children March.* Boston: Houghton Mifflin Harcourt, 2018.

The Book Itch

by Vaunda Micheaux Nelson   Grades 2–6

Summary

"All kinds of people came to 2107, 7th Avenue – kids and grown-ups, black folks and white folks, writers and politicians…even famous people" (page 3). The National Memorial African Bookstore was started in Harlem Square by Lewis Henri Micheaux. It was a bookstore for black people, which started out as a push-cart through the streets of Harlem. Read this amazing story to find out all about this bookstore with a "zillion" books, which was visited by countless people over the forty-plus years it was in existence.

Nelson, Vaunda Micheaux. *The Book Itch.* Minneapolis: CarolRhoda Books, 2015.

Questions for discussion, written responses, and/or research

1. The bookstore owner's son worked at the store on weekends and in the summer. What were some of his responsibilities?

2. What does the expression, "Dad got the book itch and needed to scratch it" (page 7) mean?

3. When Dad went to the bank to borrow money for the bookstore, what did the banker tell him? Why was this a racist comment?

4. Despite being turned down by the bank, Dad worked to save money to buy the bookstore. What type of work did he do?

5. Dad had some favorite expressions like "Knowledge is power. You need it every hour," and "You are not necessarily a fool because you didn't go to school" (pages 11–12). What did he mean by each expression? How did he react to his son's suggestion that he not go to school? What did Dad say to little Lewis?

6. Another favorite expression of Dad's was "Don't stop asking questions." Why did he give this advice to his son?

7. Dad believed that not everything you read is true. What did Dad say would help little Lewis determine if something he read was true or not?

8. Why did Dad let people who came to his bookstore read without always buying a book?

9. Why did Dad call the bookstore "The House of Common Sense and the Home of Proper Propaganda" (page 15)?

10. The bookstore had a raised platform outside. What was it for?

11. Why were there frequently police cars outside of the bookstore? How was this racist?

12. Who was Malcolm X? What happened to him?

13. What were Dad's beliefs about Malcolm X's teachings, despite what happened to him?

Select related children's literature

Weatherford, Carole Boston. *Schomburg: The Man Who Built a Library.* Somerville, MA: Candlewick Press, 2017.

Martin And Mahalia: His Words, Her Song

by Andrea Davis Pinkney
and Brian Pinkney   Grades 3–6

Summary

Martin Luther King, Jr. preached the gospel at Ebenezer Baptist Church in Atlanta, Georgia. Mahalia Jackson sang gospel music in her church in New Orleans, Louisiana. They used their loud voices to preach and sing the gospel, respectively. They lived during a time when "separate never equal" was practiced. Jim Crow laws ensured this in the South, where whites and blacks could not drink from the same water fountains, attend the same theaters, or go to the same schools. Each of them was an activist for civil rights for equality of all people. Martin's oratory excited people, and Mahalia's singing inspired people. Read the book to find out how Martin and Mahalia united at the March on Washington to create a better world where all people could be free.

Pinkney, Andrea Davis and Pinkney, Brian. *Martin and Mahalia: His Words, Her Song*. New York: Little, Brown and Company Books for Young Readers, 2013.

Questions for discussion, written responses, and/or research

1. What were the Jim Crow laws? Who was directly affected by these laws? You may have to do some research to answer these questions.

2. How did Martin Luther King, Jr. and Mahalia Jackson each use their voice to spread the message about equal rights and freedom?

3. When did Mahalia and Martin start working together? Under which circumstances? What was the outcome?

4. Martin and Mahalia were trailblazers. What does this mean? What did they do?

5. What was the March on Washington? When did it occur? What was its purpose?

6. Martin and Mahalia championed nonviolence even when encountering violence. Why did they have this belief?

7. The crowd of thousands gathered at the Lincoln Memorial. How did Martin Luther King, Jr. get their attention when he was ready to give his "I Have a Dream" speech?

8. The illustrations in this book support the story, especially those showing the throngs of people who came to hear Martin speak. How is this event depicted in the illustration?

9. Read through the timeline at the end of the book and discuss some of the highlights of Martin and Mahalia's journey.

Select related children's literature:

Nolan, Nina. *Mahalia Jackson*. New York: Amistad, 2015.

Harlem Renaissance Party

by Faith Ringgold   Grades 3–6

Summary

Noted author and illustrator Faith Ringgold takes us on a historical journey through the Harlem Renaissance of the 1920s and 1930s, with Uncle Bates and Lonnie accompanying the reader on their journey. The book introduces the reader to famous musicians, poets, activists, scholars, and others as it describes the Harlem Renaissance and why it was so important to the history of black America.

Ringgold, Faith. *Harlem Renaissance Party.* New York: Amistad, 2015.

Questions for discussion, written responses, and/or research

1. Where is Harlem?

2. The first person Lonnie met on his imaginary trip was Jack Johnson. What was he famous for?

3. What achievements were made by W.E.B. Du Bois?

4. How did Uncle Bates explain why this period was called the Harlem Renaissance?

5. What is the NAACP? Who was a founder of this organization?

6. Where is the NAACP located today? Who is the national president? Use Google to find out.

7. Who were some of the artists of the Harlem Renaissance?

8. Why did Uncle Bates say, "Your Aunt Connie taught me that this art shows the true beauty of black people. It is as if we were invisible before these artists painted us black" (page 15)?

9. Who was Madam C.J. Walker? Why was she famous?

10. Who are some of the musicians Lonnie met on his imaginary trip?

11. Use Google to find out where the Schomburg Library was. Which famous author did Lonnie meet at the Schomburg?

12. Who was Carter Woodson? What is he known for that we celebrate today?

13. Who was Satchmo? How did he get this name?

14. What did Lonnie say about why the Harlem Renaissance was so important?

15. Google Faith Ringgold and write a summary of her life and accomplishments.

If A Bus Could Talk

by Faith Ringgold   Grades 1–4

Summary

Marcie is waiting at the bus stop for her bus to take her to school, but something unusual happens. A special bus arrives, full of people, but lacking a driver. Is the bus speaking to her? Marcie sits in a special seat reserved for Rosa Parks, civil rights activist, for whom the bus is named. She is asked to move to a different seat since once a year Rosa's seat is reserved for her. While riding to school, Marcie learns all about Rosa Parks and how she made it possible for black people to ride the bus, sit at lunch counters with white people, earn the right to vote, and so many other freedoms previously assigned to whites only.

Ringgold, Faith. *If a Bus Could Talk*. New York: Aladdin, 1999.

Questions for discussion, written responses, and/or research

1. Rosa McCauley was born on February 4, 1913. At the young age of two, her mother took her and her baby brother to Pine Level, Alabama, to work on their grandfather's farm. Why did their father not go with them?

2. Who was the Ku Klux Klan? Why were Rosa, her brother, and her mom afraid of them?

3. Rosa disliked how white people treated black people. How did she deal with a white boy who threatened to punch her?

4. Rosa went to a black school, in which there was one teacher for fifty-plus students. How else was the black school different from the white school?

5. What sacrifices did her mother, Leona, make so Rosa could attend a better school?

6. Rosa later graduated from high school, but could not immediately find a job in her field so she worked at a department store. What skills did she have when she graduated?

7. What happened to Rosa when she boarded a bus from home to work? What did she have to do to get to her job? Why did this happen?

8. Why were buses a form of segregation? Where were black people allowed to sit?

9. Rosa married Raymond Parks and joined the NAACP, where her husband had been a long-time member. What is the NAACP? What types of things did Rosa do while a member of the NAACP?

10. What happened to Rosa on December 1, 1955? How did she react? What happened to her as a result of her reaction?

11. How did Rosa meet Dr. Martin Luther King, Jr.?

12. What was the Montgomery Bus Boycott? Was it successful? How long did it last?

13. What were some of the injustices done to black people as a result of the Montgomery Bus Boycott?

14. What happened on November 15, 1956?

15. Rosa's work for equal rights continued. List some of Rosa's accomplishments.

16. What awards did Rosa Parks earn during her lifetime?

17. What did you learn from this story?

We Came To America

by Faith Ringgold   Grades K–5

Summary

America is a melting pot, a country rich in diversity. Meet some of the people who came to America, and those who were already here when others arrived. A beautifully illustrated and well-written book in poetic form.

Ringgold, Faith. *We Came to America*. New York: Alfred A. Knopf, 2016.

Questions for discussion, written responses, and/or research

1. Who were the people who were already in America when others came?

2. Some people came in chains. Who were these people? In what ways did they lose their "freedom and their names" (page 4)? Why did this happen?

3. "Every color, race and religion" (page 1) came to America. What does this mean?

4. Do you know anyone who wasn't born in America? Where did they come from?

5. How did they travel to America?

6. Why did some of these people leave their homelands?

7. We still have people who come to America. We call this immigration. What do you hear about immigration in the news? What are some of the reasons that people today leave their birthplace?

8. Name some of the things people brought with them when they came from other countries.

9. What is the important message of this story?

Justice Makes A Difference

by Dr. Artika Tyner
and Jacklyn Milton   Grades 5–8

Summary

Justice loved visiting her grandma's house. Grandma had a wonderful library of books through which she traveled the world, inspiring her granddaughter to learn through reading as well. They spent many afternoons together in the library reading. Throughout this story, we learn about many African Americans in history who had a profound influence on civil rights, racial equality, black freedom, and music. The story creates the impression that the author's and Justice's lives are running in parallel.

Tyner, Dr. Artika and Milton, Jacklyn. *Justice Makes a Difference*. St. Paul, MN: Planting People Growing Justice Press, 2017.

Questions for discussion, written responses, and/or research

1. The story states that Justice's grandma always makes her feel important. What are some of the ways Grandma does this? How else can you make someone feel important?

2. Grandma told Justice that her name had a lot of responsibility associated with it. Why did she say that? What type of responsibility did Grandma mean?

3. Name some of the things Grandma did to "make a difference" in the world.

4. Which things did Grandma tell Justice she had already done and could do to make a difference?

5. Many African-American historical figures are mentioned in the book for the differences they have made. Who are some of these people? How did each contribute to making a better world for African Americans?

6. Who was Dr. Wangari Maathai? What did she accomplish? How did her accomplishments inspire Justice to start a community project?

7. When Justice came home from school one day and was upset because other kids told her that women can't be president, what did Grandma do?

8. Do some research to find out who Shirley Chisholm was, and discuss your findings with your class.

9. Justice learned that there was a legal case entitled Brown vs. Board of Education. What was this case about? What was the outcome?

10. After reading so many books and having so many conversations with her grandma, Justice decided on what she wanted to be. What was this profession? Why did she want to pursue it?

11. At the end of the book are some brief biographies of African-American leaders who inspired the book. Read about these great people and do some further research into their lives and accomplishments.

The Teachers March! How Selma's Teachers Changed History

by Sandra Neil Wallace
and Rich Wallace   Grades 4–8

Summary

Fighting for the right to vote, Selma's teachers, led by Reverend F.D. Reese, marched to the courthouse in Selma, Alabama, to register to vote. Selma was a segregated community – white people were kept apart from black people. The sheriff of Selma and his deputies were determined to block the marchers from entering the courthouse and registering to vote. To oppose the teachers' right to vote, a law was declared prohibiting them from marching and speaking about voting rights. In the end, with the help of Reverend Reese and Dr. Martin Luther King, Jr., the teachers prevailed and the Voting Rights Act of 1965 passed Congress.

Wallace, Sandra Neil and Wallace, Rich. *The Teachers March! How Selma's Teachers Changed History*. New York: Calkins Creek, 2020.

Questions for discussion, written responses, and/or research

1. Reverend F.D. Reese, a high school science teacher, believed every citizen was a first-class citizen. Which federal document supports his belief? What did this document guarantee for all citizens?

2. Selma, Alabama, was a segregated city. What does this mean?

3. The sheriff of Selma did everything to keep black people from voting. What were some of the tactics the sheriff and his deputies used against black people?

4. Reverend F.D. Reese frequently led groups of voters to the courthouse to try to register to vote, without success. Why did he think the teachers' march would be successful?

5. Teachers were unsure of whether they wanted to march because of potential problems from the sheriff and his staff, who were white. What convinced them to march? What happened after the first march?

6. Who was Dr. Martin Luther King? How was he instrumental in bringing the right to vote to all people of Selma and of the United States?

7. Why did the teachers bring toothbrushes and sandwiches to the march?

8. What were some of the other consequences for the teachers if they marched?

9. Once the teachers reached the courthouse, they were met by the sheriff and his deputies, who told the teachers to clear all the steps. The teachers resisted. What was the outcome?

10. Why were the teachers afraid of the superintendent? What problems would the superintendent encounter if he did what the teachers feared he would do?

11. Did the teachers get to register to vote as a result of this march? How did they make civil rights history?

12. What inspired other groups of people to start marching? Name some of the groups that marched.

13. Once all people had the right to vote as a result of the Voting Rights Act of 1965, what did the Selma teachers do?

14. Google the civil rights movement. With a partner, write down ten facts you found. Discuss with the class.

Select related children's literature

ACLU. *We Are the Change: Words of Inspiration from Civil Rights Leaders.* San Francisco: Chronicle Books, 2019.

Allen, Tessa. *Sometimes People March.* New York: Balzer and Bray, 2020.

Carrigan, Mellonee. *Carol Moseley-Braun: Breaking Barriers.* Chicago: Children's Press, 1994.

Frith, Margaret. *Who Was Woodrow Wilson?* New York: Penguin Random House, 2015.

Grant, Kesha. *Women in the Civil Rights Movement.* New York: Scholastic, 2020.

Grimes, Nikki. *Kamala Harris: Rooted in Justice.* New York: Atheneum Books for Young Readers, 2020.

Hooks, Gwendolyn. *If You Were a Kid During the Civil Rights Movement.* New York: Scholastic, 2017.

Millender, Dharathula. *History's All Stars: Martin Luther King, Jr.* New York: Aladdin, 2014.

Rosenstock, Barb. *Fight of the Century: Alice Paul Battles Woodrow Wilson for the Vote.* New York: Calkins Creek, 2020.

The Roots Of Rap

by Carole Boston Weatherford   Grades 3–8

Summary

An introduction to the sounds and artists of hip-hop and rap music, written as a poem and beautifully illustrated, this book provides the history of both these genres and the artists who made them great. There is a "Who's Who of Hip-Hop" at the end of the book and a glossary of commonly used terms related to hip-hop and rap.

Weatherford, Carole Boston. *The Roots of Rap*. New York: Little Bee Books, 2019.

Questions for discussion, written responses, and/or research

1. The title, *The Roots of Rap*, gives us a clue as to what this book is about. What do you think the purpose of the book is?

2. What does the author say about where rap and hip-hop came from?

3. In what decade did the rappers perform?

4. What is graffiti? Have you seen any? Where?

5. What risks do graffiti artists take?

6. Where are Manhattan, Queens, Bronx, and Brooklyn? The author refers to them as "line." What does she mean? How is this related to graffiti?

7. What is breakdancing? Use Google to find out. Have you ever seen breakdancing? Where have you seen it?

8. Why do you think breakdancers use a stage made out of cardboard?

9. What is dub? Who invented it? Have you heard it? Where?

10. Who is DJ Kool Herc? What is he famous for?

11. Search the back of this book to find out who LL Cool J, Kurtis Blow, Biggie, the Fat Boys, Ice Cube, Dr. Dre, and 50 Cent are.

12. What is hip-hop?

13. Who is Queen Latifah? What is her birth name? Google her to find out how she got her stage name, Queen Latifah.

14. Why is hip-hop and rap so important to black culture?

15. Summarize what you learned from the story.

Select related children's literature

Scott-Curran, Sara and Scott-Curran, Stewart. *A Kids Book About Creativity.* Portland, OR: A Kids Book About, Inc., 2019.

Bibliography

Abdul-Jabbar, Kareem and Obstfeld, Raymond. *What Color Is My World?: The Lost History of African-American Inventors.* Somerville, MA: Candlewick Press, 2012.

ACLU. *We Are the Change: Words of Inspiration from Civil Rights Leaders.* San Francisco: Chronicle Books, 2019.

Adero, Malika. *A Black Woman Did That.* New York: Downtown Bookworks, 2019.

Alexander, Kwame et al. *Out of Wonder.* Somerville, MA: Candlewick Press, 2017.

Alexander, Kwame and Nelson, Kadir. *The Undefeated.* New York: Houghton Mifflin Harcourt, 2019.

Alexander, Rebecca. *A Kids Book About Body Image.* Portland, OR: A Kids Book About, Inc., 2019.

Aliki. *A Weed Is a Flower: The Life of George Washington Carver.* New York: Aladdin, 1988.

Allen, Debbie. *Dancing in the Wings.* New York: Puffin Books, 2000.

Allen, Tessa. *Sometimes People March.* New York: Balzer and Bray, 2020.

Allman, John Robert. *Boys Dance!* New York: Doubleday, 2020.

Anderson, Beth. *Lizzie Demands a Seat!* New York: Calkins Creek, 2020.

Andrews, Troy. *Trombone Shorty.* New York: Abrams, 2015.

Angelou, Maya and Basquiat, Jean-Michel. *Life Doesn't Frighten Me.* New York: Abrams, 1993.

Asim, Jabari. *A Child's Introduction to African American History.* New York: Black Dog and Leventhal Publishers, 2018.

Barnes, Derrick and James, Gordon C. *Crown: An Ode to the Fresh Cut.* Chicago: Bolden, 2017.

———. *I Am Every Good Thing.* New York: Penguin Random House, 2020.

Barnes, Derrick and Brantley-Newton, Vanessa. *The King of Kindergarten.* New York: Nancy Paulson Books, 2019.

Barton, Chris. *What Do You Do With a Voice Like That? The Story of Extraordinary Congresswoman Barbara Jordan.* New York: Beach Lane Books, 2018.

Beaumont, Karen. *I Like Myself!* Boston: Houghton Mifflin Harcourt, 2006.

Becker, Helaine. *Counting on Katherine: How Katherine Johnson Saved Apollo 13.* New York: Henry Holt and Company, 2018.

Beckner, Chrisanne. *100 African Americans Who Shaped American History.* San Mateo, CA: Bluewood Books, 1995.

Benge, Janet and Benge, Geoff. *George Washington Carver: From Slave to Scientist.* Lynnwood, WA: Emerald Books, 2001.

Berman, Kathleen Cornell. *Birth of the Cool.* Salem, MA: Page Street Kids, 2019.

Black, Donnette. *Madam C.J. Walker's Road to Success.* Bloomington: AuthorHouse, 2010.

Blumenthal, Deborah. *Fancy Party Gowns.* New York: Little Bee Books, 2017.

Bridges, Ruby. *This Is Your Time.* New York: Delacorte Press, 2020.

Browne, Mahogany L. et al. *WOKE.* New York: Roaring Book Press, 2020.

Bryan, Ashley. *Beautiful Blackbird.* New York: Atheneum Books for Young Readers, 2003.

Bryan, Zahra. *Black Girl Magic.* Fort Lauderdale: Arhaz Nyleak, 2020.

Bryer, H.T. *Hidden Genius: Frank Mann, the Black Engineer Behind Howard Hughes.* Oak Harbor, OH: Grey Forest Press, 2011.

Buckley, James Jr. *Who Was Jesse Owens?* New York: Penguin Random House, 2015.

Burk, Rachelle. *The Story of Simone Biles.* Emeryville, CA: Rockledge Press, 2020.

Byers, Grace. *I Am Enough.* New York: Balzer and Bray, 2018.

———. *I Believe I Can.* New York: Balzer and Bray, 2020.

Calkhoven, Laurie. *Lin-Manuel Miranda.* New York: Simon Spotlight, 2018.

Carrigan, Mellonee. *Carol Moseley-Braun: Breaking Barriers.* Chicago: Children's Press, 1994.

Carroll, Kevin. *A Kids Book About Belonging.* Portland, OR: A Kids Book About, Inc., 2019.

Carter, Andy and Saller, Carol. *George Washington Carver.* Minneapolis: Millbrook Press, 2001.

Celano, Marianne et al. *Something Happened in Our Town.* Washington, D.C.: Magination Press, 2018.

Chambers, Veronica. *Shirley Chisholm Is a Verb.* New York: Dial Books for Young Readers, 2020.

Chambers, Veronica and the Staff of the New York Times. *Finish the Fight.* New York: Houghton Mifflin Harcourt, 2020.

Charles, Tami. *All Because You Matter.* New York: Orchard Books, 2020.

Chen, Eva. *A Is For Awesome! 23 Iconic Women Who Changed the World.* New York: Macmillan, 2019.

Cherry, Matthew A. *Hair Love.* New York: Penguin Random House, 2019.

Clinton, Chelsea. *She Persisted Around the World: 13 Women Who Changed History.* New York: Philomel Books, 2018.

———. *She Persisted in Sports: American Olympians Who Changed the World.* New York: Philomel Books, 2020.

———. *She Persisted: 13 American Women Who Changed the World.* New York: Philomel Books, 2017.

Copeland, Misty. *Black Ballerinas.* New York: Aladdin, 2021.

———. *Bunheads.* New York: Penguin Random House, 2020.

———. *Firebird.* New York: G.P. Putnam, 2014.

Cornwall, Gaia. *Jabari Tries.* Somerville, MA: Candlewick Press, 2019.

Curcio, Anthony. *The Boy Who Became King: LeBron James.* Columbia, SC: Anthony Curcio, 2021.

———. *The Boy Who Never Gave Up: Stephen Curry.* www.sportivabooks.com, 2018.

Curry, Parker and Curry, Jessica. *Parker Looks Up.* New York: Simon and Schuster, 2019.

———. *Parker Shines On.* New York: Aladdin, 2021.

Denise, Anika Aldamuy. *Planting Stories.* New York: HarperCollins, 2019.

BIBLIOGRAPHY

Diehn, Andi. *Computer Decoder: Dorothy Vaughan.* White River Junction, VT: Nomad Press, 2019.

Diggs, Taye. *Mixed Me!* New York: Macmillan, 2015.

Domoney, Cathy. *The Magic Is Inside You.* North Charleston, SC: Cathy Domoney, 2011.

Dougherty, Rachel. *Secret Engineer.* New York: Roaring Book, 2020.

Duncan, Alice Faye. *A Song for Gwendolyn Brooks.* New York: Sterling Children's Books, 2019.

———. *Memphis, Martin and the Mountaintop.* New York: Calkins Creek, 2018.

Easton, Emily. *Enough!* New York: Crown Books for Young Readers, 2018.

Elliot, Zetta. *A Place Inside of Me.* New York: Farrar, Straus and Giroux, 2020.

Engle, Margarita. *Dancing Hands.* New York: Atheneum Books for Young Readers, 2019.

Engle, Susan. *Robert Sengstacke Abbott: A Man, a Paper, and a Parade.* Wilmette, IL: Bellwood, 2019.

Evans-Ford, Argrow (Kit). *Bishop Richard Allen: A Nonviolent Journey.* n.p., IL: Testimonies of Hope Press, 2014.

Feiner, Beck. *American Legends Alphabet.* Memphis, TN: Alphabet Legends Pty Ltd., 2018.

———. *Autistic Legends Alphabet.* Memphis, TN: Alphabet Legends Pty Ltd., 2019.

———. *Baseball Legends Alphabet.* Memphis, TN: Alphabet Legends Pty Ltd., 2019.

———. *Basketball Legends Alphabet.* Memphis, TN: Alphabet Legends Pty Ltd., 2019.

———. *Dance Legends Alphabet.* Memphis, TN: Alphabet Legends Pty Ltd., 2019.

———. *Dyslexia Legends Alphabet.* Memphis, TN: Alphabet Legends Pty Ltd., 2019.

———. *Football Legends Alphabet.* Memphis, TN: Alphabet Legends Pty Ltd., 2019.

———. *Lady Legends Alphabet.* Memphis, TN: Alphabet Legends Pty Ltd., 2018.

———. *Liberty Legends Alphabet.* Memphis, TN: Alphabet Legends Pty Ltd., 2019.

———. *Little Legends Alphabet.* Memphis, TN: Alphabet Legends Pty Ltd., 2018.

———. *Sports Women Legends Alphabet.* Memphis, TN: Alphabet Legends Pty Ltd., 2019.

Fishman, Jon. *Gabby Douglas.* Minneapolis: Lerner, 2013.

Frith, Margaret. *Who Was Woodrow Wilson?* New York: Penguin Random House, 2015.

Gaines, Joanna. *The World Needs Who You Were Made to Be.* Nashville: Tommy Nelson, 2020.

Giovanni, Nicki. *I Am Loved.* New York: HarperCollins, 2018.

Goldenbock, Peter. *Hank Aaron: Brave in Every Way.* Orlando: Houghton Mifflin Harcourt, 2001.

Golio, Gary. *Strange Fruit: Billie Holiday and the Power of a Protest Song.* Minneapolis: Millbrook Press, 2017.

Gordon, Charnaie. *A Kids Book About Diversity.* Portland, OR: A Kids Book About, Inc., 2021.

Gorman, Amanda. *Change Sings.* New York: Viking Press, 2021.

Goss, Nathalie and Goss, Alex. *We All Belong.* n.p.: Goss Castle, 2020.

Grant, Kesha. *Women in the Civil Rights Movement.* New York: Scholastic, 2020.

Greenfield, Eloise. *Mary McLeod Bethune.* New York: HarperCollins, 1977.

Griffin, Molly Beth. *Ten Beautiful Things.* Watertown, MA: Charlesbridge, 2021.

Grimes, Nikki. *Kamala Harris: Rooted in Justice.* New York: Atheneum Books for Young Readers, 2020.

———. *Legacy.* New York: Bloomsbury Children's Books, 2021.

———. *One Last Word.* New York: Bloomsbury Children's Books, 2017.

Hall, Carla. *Carla and the Christmas Cornbread.* New York: Simon and Schuster, 2021.

Haquet, Alice Brière. *Nina.* Watertown, MA: Charlesbridge, 2017.

Harrington, Janice. *Buzzing with Questions: The Inquisitive Mind of Charles Henry Turner.* Honesdale, PA: Calkins Creek, 2019.

Harris, Brian Keith II. *I Am My History.* n.p.: Brian Keith Harris, 2020.

Harris, Kamala. *Superheroes Are Everywhere.* New York: Philomel Books, 2019.

Harris, Meena. *Ambitious Girl.* New York: Little, Brown and Company Books for Young Readers, 2021.

———. *Kamala and Maya's Big Idea.* New York: HarperCollins, 2020.

Harrison, Vashti. *Little Dreamers: Visionary Women Around the World.* New York: Little, Brown and Company Books for Young Readers, 2018.

———. *Little Leaders: Bold Women in Black History.* New York: Little, Brown and Company Books for Young Readers, 2017.

Harvey, Jeanne Walker. *My Hands Sing The Blues.* Las Vegas: Amazon Children's Publishing, 2011.

Herman, Steve. *Different Is Not Bad.* Houston, TX: My Dragon Books, 2020.

Hernandez, Laurie. *She's Got This.* New York: HarperCollins, 2018.

Hicks, Dr. Laymon. *A Kids Book About Failure.* Portland, OR: A Kids Book About, Inc., 2019.

Higginbotham, Anastasia. *Not My Idea.* New York: Dottir Press, 2018.

Higginson, Sheila Sweeny. *Kids Who Are Changing the World.* New York: Simon Spotlight, 2019.

Hill, Laban Carrick. *When the Beat Was Born.* New York: Roaring Brook, 2013.

Hood, Susan. *Shaking Things Up. 14 Young Women Who Changed the World.* New York: HarperCollins, 2018.

Hooks, Gwendolyn. *If You Were a Kid During the Civil Rights Movement.* New York: Scholastic, 2017.

———. *Tiny Stitches.* New York: Lee and Low, 2016.

Hopkinson, Deborah. *Carter Reads the Newspaper.* Atlanta: Peachtree, 2019.

———. *What Is the Women's Right Movement?* New York: Penguin Random House, 2018.

Hubbard, Christine. *Arthur Ashe.* New York: Lee and Low, 2018.

Hubbard, Rita Lorraine. *The Oldest Student: How May Hubbard Learned to Read.* New York: Schwartz and Wade Books, 2020.

Hudson, Cheryl Willis. *Brave. Black. First.* New York: Penguin Random House, 2020.

Issa, Kai Jackson. *Howard Thurman's Great Hope.* New York: Lee and Low, 2008.

Jaffe, Elizabeth. *Ellen Ochoa.* New York: Children's Press, 2004.

James, LeBron. *I Promise.* New York: HarperCollins, 2020.

Jeffrey, Gary. *Thurgood Marshall: The Supreme Court Rules on "Separate but Equal".* New York: Gareth Stevens Publishing, 2013.

Johnson, Angela. *A Girl Like Me.* Minneapolis: Millbrook Press, 2004.

Jones, Lynda. *Five Brilliant Scientists.* New York: Scholastic, 2000.

Jordan, Deloris and Jordan, Roslyn M. *Salt in His Shoes.* New York: Aladdin, 2000.

Joseph, Jayla. *What Will I Be?* Coppell, TX: Independently Published, 2020.

Joy, Angela. *Black Is a Rainbow Color.* New York: Roaring Book Press, 2020.

Kay, Meir. *A Kids Book About Optimism.* Portland, OR: A Kids Books About, Inc., 2020.

Keats, Ezra Jack. *The Snowy Day.* New York: Viking Press, 1962.

Kenyon, Ben. *A Kids Book About Gratitude.* Portland, OR: A Kids Book About, Inc., 2019.

Killiebrew, J. *There Is a Girl Headed to the White House.* n.p., U.S.: Dr. Jazz Killiebrew, Ph.D., 2020.

Kinew, Wab. *Go Show the World.* New York: Tundra, 2018.

King, Shani Mahiri. *Have I Ever Told You Black Lives Matter.* Thomaston, ME: Tilbury House, 2021.

Kirkfield, Vivian. *Sweet Dreams, Sarah*. Berkeley, CA: Creston Books, 2019.

Krull, Kathleen. *Harvesting Hope. The Story of Cesar Chavez*. Boston: Houghton Mifflin Harcourt, 2003.

———. *Wilma Unlimited*. New York: Houghton Mifflin Harcourt, 1996.

Kudlinski, Kathleen. *Rosa Parks*. New York: Aladdin, 2001.

Labrecque, Ellen. *Who Was Kobe Bryant?* New York: Penguin Random House, 2020.

———. *Who Was Maya Angelou?* New York: Penguin Random House, 2016.

Langley, Sharon and Nathan, Amy. *A Ride to Remember*. New York: Abrams, 2020.

Lasky, Kathryn. *A Voice of Her Own*. Somerville, MA: Candlewick Press, 2003.

Latham, Irene and Waters, Charles. *Can I Touch Your Hair?* Minneapolis: CarolRhoda Press, 2018.

Leannah, Michael. *Most Days*. Thomaston, ME: Tilbury House, 2021.

———. *Most People*. Maine: Tilbury House, 2017.

Leslie, Tonya. *The Story of John Lewis*. Emeryville, CA: Rockridge Press, 2021.

Levinson, Cynthia. *The Youngest Marcher: The Story of Audrey Faye Hendricks, a Young Civil Rights Activist*. New York: Atheneum Books for Young Readers, 2017.

Levy, Debbie. *I Dissent: Ruth Bader Ginsburg Makes Her Mark*. New York: Simon and Schuster, 2016.

Lyon, George Ella. *Voices of Justice*. New York: Henry Holt and Company, 2020.

Lyons, Kelly Starling. *Dream Builder: The Story of Architect Philip Freelon*. New York: Lee and Low, 2020.

————. *Sing a Song*. New York: Nancy Paulson Books, 2019.

Macnalie, Joa. *The Hero in the Helmet: Colin Kaepernick*. Lewes, DE: Melanin Origins, 2018.

Mahin, Michael. *Muddy: The Story of Blues Legend Muddy Waters*. New York: Atheneum Books for Young Readers, 2017.

Marshall, Akura. *Gary and the Great Inventors*. Burlington, ON: Our Children's Network, Inc., 2018.

Masi, Dawn. *G My Name is Girl*. New York: Doubleday, 2021.

McDonough, Yona Zeldis. *Who Was Louis Armstrong?* New York: Penguin Random House, 2004.

McGregor, Leesa. *A New Alphabet for Humanity*. n.p.: Impact for Humanity Publishing, 2019.

McKissack, Patricia. *What is Given from The Heart*. New York: Penguin Random House, 2019.

McLaurin, Patrice. *Have You Thanked an Inventor Today?* Lawrenceville, GA: Khemrah Publishing, 2016.

Mellage, Nanette. *Coming Home: A Story of Josh Gibson, Baseball's Greatest Home Run Hitter*. Mahwah, NJ: Bridgewater Books, 2001.

Memory, Jelani. *A Kids Book About Racism*. Portland, OR: A Kids Book About, Inc., 2019.

Millender, Dharathula. *History's All Stars: Martin Luther King, Jr.* New York: Aladdin, 2014.

Miller, Pat Zeitlow. *The Quickest Kid in Clarksville*. San Francisco: Chronicle Books, 2016.

Miller, William. *Zora Hurston and the Chinaberry Tree*. New York: Lee and Low, 1994.

Morgan, Caverly. *A Kids Book About Mindfulness*. Portland, OR: A Kids Book About, Inc., 2020.

Morgan, Sally J. *Simone Biles: Golden Girl of Gymnastics*. New York: Penguin Random House, 2020.

Mosca, Julia Finley. *The Astronaut with a Song for the Stars: The Story of Dr. Ellen Ochoa*. Seattle: The Innovation Press, 2019.

———. *The Doctor with an Eye for Eyes: The Story of Dr. Patricia Bath*. Seattle: The Innovation Press, 2017.

———. *The Girl Who Thought in Pictures*. Seattle: The Innovation Press, 2017.

———. *The Girl with a Mind for Math: The Story of Raye Montague*. Seattle: The Innovation Press, 2018.

Moss, Caroline. *Become a Leader Like Michelle Obama*. Minneapolis: Frances Lincoln Children's Books, 2020.

———. *Blast Off into Space Like Mae Jemison*. Minneapolis: Frances Lincoln Children's Books, 2020.

Moss, Wendy. *Being Me: A Kid's Guide to Boosting Confidence and Self-Esteem*. Washington, D.C.: Magination Press, 2011.

Murphy, Frank. *A Boy Like You*. Ann Arbor, MI: Sleeping Bear Press, 2019.

Murphy, Frank and Murphy, Carla. *A Girl Like You*. Ann Arbor, MI: Sleeping Bear Press, 2020.

Napper, Kristine. *A Kids Book About Disabilities*. Portland, OR: A Kids Book About, Inc., 2020.

Nelson, Vaunda Micheaux. *The Book Itch*. Minneapolis: CarolRhoda Books, 2015.

Next Up. *A Kids Book About Voting*. Portland, OR: A Kids Book About, Inc., 2020.

Nolan, Nina. *Mahalia Jackson*. New York: Amistad, 2015.

Nyong'o, Lupita. *Sulwe*. New York: Simon and Schuster, 2019.

Ochiltree, Dianne. *Molly, by Golly!* New York: Calkins Creek, 2012.

O'Neal, Shaquille. *Little Shaq Takes a Chance*. New York: Bloomsbury, 2016.

Orgill, Roxanne. *If I Only Had a Horn*. Boston: Houghton Mifflin Harcourt, 1997.

Ortiz, Simon J. *The People Shall Continue*. New York: Children's Book Press, 1988.

Oz, Shola. *I Am Whole*. London: I Am Whole Books, 2020.

Palacio, R.J. *Share Your Rainbow*. New York: Penguin Random House, 2020.

Pellum, Kimberly Brown. *Black Women in Science*. Emeryville, CA: Rockledge Press, 2019.

Perry, Latasha M. *Skin Like Mine*. Grand Blanc, MI: Kids Like Mine, 2016.

Pew Research. "Views on Race in America: Social and Demographic Trends." 2019. www.pewresearch.org

Pimental, Annette Bay. *All the Way to the Top*. Naperville, IL: Sourcebook eXplore, 2020.

Pinkney, Andrea Davis. *Alvin Ailey*. Los Angeles: Hyperion, 1993.

———. *Duke Ellington*. New York: Hyperion, 1998.

———. *Ella Fitzgerald*. New York: Disney Jump at the Sun, 2002.

———. *The Red Pencil*. New York: Little, Brown and Company Books for Young Readers, 2014.

Pinkney, Andrea Davis and Pinkney, Brian. *Martin and Mahalia: His Words, Her Song*. New York: Little, Brown and Company Books for Young Readers, 2013.

Powell, Patricia Hruby. *Josephine*. San Francisco: Chronicle Books, 2014.

———. *Lift as You Climb: The Story of Ella Baker*. New York: Simon and Schuster, 2020.

Ransome, Lisa Cline. *Before She Was Harriet*. New York: Holiday House, 2017.

———. *The Power of Her Pen*. New York: Simon and Schuster, 2020.

Reid, Megan. *Maryam's Magic*. New York: HarperCollins, 2021.

Rhodes-Pitts, Sharifa. *Jake Makes a World*. New York: MoMA, 2015.

Rich, Francine Poppo. *Larry Bird*. West Bay Shore, NY: Blue Martin, 2009.

Ringgold, Faith. *Harlem Renaissance Party*. New York: Amistad, 2015.

———. *If a Bus Could Talk*. New York: Aladdin, 1999.

———. *We Came to America*. New York: Alfred A. Knopf, 2016.

Roberts, Daron. *A Kids Book About Empathy*. Portland, OR: A Kids Book About, Inc., 2020.

Robeson, Theresa. *Queen of Physics*. New York: Sterling, 2019.

Robinson, Monica Clark. *Let the Children March*. Boston: Houghton Mifflin Harcourt, 2018.

———. *Standing on Her Shoulders: A Celebration of Women*. New York: Orchard Books, 2021.

Rodriguez, Ayesha. *I Am ... Positive Affirmations for Brown Boys*. www.ayesharodriguez.com, 2016.

Romito, Dee. *Pies from Nowhere*. New York: Little Bee Books, 2018.

Rosenstock, Barb. *Fight of the Century: Alice Paul Battles Woodrow Wilson for the Vote.* New York: Calkins Creek, 2020.

Rusch, Elizabeth. *Mario and the Hole in the Sky.* Watertown, MA: Charlesbridge, 2019.

Russell-Brown, Katheryn. *Little Melba and Her Big Trombone.* New York: Lee and Low, 2014.

Ryan, Pam Muñoz. *When Marian Sang.* New York: Scholastic, 2002.

Sanders, Joshunda. *I Can Write the World.* Houston: Six Foot Press, 2019.

Scott-Curran, Sara and Scott-Curran, Stewart. *A Kids Book About Creativity.* Portland, OR: A Kids Book About, Inc., 2019.

Shabazz, Ilyasah. *Malcolm Little.* New York: Atheneum Books for Young Readers, 2013.

Shelton, Paula Young. *Child of the Civil Rights Movement.* New York: DragonFly, 2010.

Shepherd, Crown. *Black Boy, Black Boy.* St Paul, MN: Beaver's Pond Press, 2020.

Shetterly, Margot Lee. *Hidden Figures: The True Story of Four Black Women and the Space Race.* New York: HarperCollins, 2018.

Simpson, Nakita. *A Kids Book About Emotions.* Portland, OR: A Kids Book About, Inc., 2020.

Slade, Suzanne. *June Almeida, Virus Detective.* Ann Arbor, MI: Sleeping Bear Press, 2021.

Smith, Charles R. *Black Jack: The Ballad of Jack Johnson.* New York: Roaring Books Press, 2010.

Smith, Sherri L. *Who Were the Tuskegee Airmen?* New York: Penguin Random House, 2020.

Sorell, Traci. *We Are Grateful*. Watertown, MA: Charlesbridge, 2018.

———. *We Are Still Here*. Watertown, MA: Charlesbridge, 2021.

Steptoe, Javaka. *Radiant Child: The Story of Jean-Michel Basquiat*. New York: Little, Brown and Company Books for Young Readers, 2016.

Stramwasser, Adam. *A Kids Book About Money*. Portland, OR: A Kids Book About, Inc., 2019.

Swain-Bates, Crystal. *Big Hair, Don't Care*. Walnut, CA: Goldest Karat Publishing, 2013.

Szabo, Ross. *A Kids Book About Anxiety*. Portland, OR: A Kids Book About, Inc., 2019.

Talbert, Lyn-Sisson and Talbert, David E. *The Square Root of Possible*. New York: Penguin Random House, 2020.

Tarpley, Natasha Anastasia. *I Love My Hair!* New York: Little, Brown and Company Books for Young Readers, 1998.

The Undefeated, ESPN. *The Fierce 44: Black Americans Who Shook Up the World*. Boston: Houghton Mifflin Harcourt, 2019.

Thierry, Jordan. *A Kids Book About Systemic Racism*. Portland, OR: A Kids Book About, Inc., 2020.

Tom, Elizabeth. *A Kids Book About Bullying*. Portland, OR: A Kids Book About, Inc., 2020.

Tonatiuh, Duncan. *Separate Is Never Equal*. New York: Abrams, 2014.

Tucker, Zoe. *We Are The Supremes*. London: Wide Eyed Editions, 2021.

Tyner, Dr. Artika and Milton, Jacklyn. *Justice Makes a Difference*. St. Paul, MN: Planting People Growing Justice Press, 2017.

Underwood, Deborah. *Outside in*. Boston: Houghton Mifflin Harcourt, 2020.

Vegara, Maria Isabel Sanchez. *Aretha Franklin*. London: Frances Lincoln Children's Books, 2020.

———. *Ella Fitzgerald*. London: Frances Lincoln, 2017.

———. *Frida Kahlo*. London: Frances Lincoln, 2016.

———. *Jean-Michel Basquiat*. London: Frances Lincoln, 2020.

———. *Prince*. London: Frances Lincoln, 2021.

Verde, Susan. *Hey Wall*. New York: Simon and Schuster, 2018.

Wadsworth, Ginger. *Benjamin Banneker*. Minneapolis: Millbrook Press, 2003.

Wallace, Sandra Neil and Wallace, Rich. *The Teachers March! How Selma's Teachers Changed History*. New York: Calkins Creek, 2020.

Watson, Renee. *Harlem's Little Blackbird*. New York: Penguin Random House, 2012.

Weatherford, Carole Boston. *Before John Was a Jazz Giant*. New York: Henry Holt and Company, 2008.

———. *Gordon Parks*. Chicago: Albert Whitman, 2015.

———. *Leontyne Price*. New York: Alfred Knopf, 2014.

———. *RESPECT: Aretha Franklin, The Queen of Soul*. New York: Atheneum Books for Young Readers, 2020.

———. *Schomburg: The Man Who Built a Library*. Somerville, MA: Candlewick Press, 2017.

———. *The Legendary Miss Lena Horne*. New York: Atheneum Books for Young Readers, 2017.

————. *The Roots of Rap*. New York: Little Bee Books, 2019.

Voice of Freedom: Fannie Lou Hamer. Somerville, MA: Candlewick Press, 2015.

Wheeler, Lisa. *Someone Builds the Dream*. New York: Dial, 2021.

White, C. Ian. *Grandpa and the Library*. New York: MoMA, 2018.

Williams, Maggy. *I'm Mixed*. Ann Arbor, MI: Loving Healing Press, 2018.

Wilson, Jamia. *Young, Gifted and Black*. Beverly, MA: Wide Eyed Editions, 2018.

Winter, Jonah. *Sonia Sotomayor*. New York: Atheneum Books for Young Readers, 2009.

Winter, Jonah and Collier, Bryan. *Lillian's Right to Vote*. New York: Penguin Random House, 2015.

————. *Thurgood*. New York: Schwartz and Wade Books, 2019.

Wittenstein, Barry. *A Place to Land*. New York: Holiday Books, 2019.

Woodson, Jacqueline. *The Day You Begin*. New York: Nancy Paulson, 2018.

————. *The Other Side*. New York: Nancy Paulson, 2001.

————. *This Is the Rope*. New York: Penguin Random House, 2013.

Wright, Richard. *Seeing into Tomorrow*. Minneapolis: Millbrook Press, 2017.

Yousafzai, Malala. *Malala's Magic Pencil*. New York: Little, Brown and Company Books for Young Readers, 2017.

Grade Index

6-8

Acknowledgments

This book would not have been possible without the love and encouragement of my best friend and husband, Bernard (Buz) for his extensive support in planning, developing scope and mission, and editing. He has been my strongest advocate throughout my career.

My children Jennifer, Joshua, Joseph, and Margaret have been cheerleaders of this project and role models in parenting their own children, Samantha, Jacob, and Nathaniel, using many of the principles of this book. It is for you and children in future generations for whom I have written this book.

A special thank you goes to Gary A. Plummer, my coauthor. Although Gary was my graduate student at Arcadia University and also became my colleague in the Philadelphia, Pennsylvania and Lower Merion

Montgomery County, Pennsylvania schools, Gary actually taught me African American history throughout these decades. Gary holds the Presidential Award for Excellence in Mathematics Teaching in Pennsylvania. Gary played an equally important role in this work.

I am most grateful to the entire Rethink Press team without whom this work could not have come together so seamlessly. Special thanks to Lucy McCarraher, Joe Gregory, Anke Ueberberg, Nkiru Asika, Jennifer Scott, Kerry Boettcher, Tess Jolly, and Kinga Stabryla.

Thanks to our friend Michael Carter, a noted entrepreneur and visionary who introduced me to Rethink Press.

Dr. Gregory M. Anderson, Dean of the College of Education and Human Development at Temple University, deserves my deep gratitude for agreeing to write the Foreword to this book.

Thanks to the many educational leaders who helped shape my career and accomplishments including Dr. David W. Magill, former superintendent of the Lower Merion School District and Director Emeritus of the University of Chicago Lab School, the late Dr. H. Bernard Miller who was my doctoral advisor, and Dr. Michael W. Smith, Professor and Chair of the Department of Teaching and Learning at Temple University.

Thanks to my lifelong friends, Lee and Barbara Michaels, for being good sounding boards throughout my work on this book and also to Maureen Wallin and Mary Kay August who have been there to handle much of the organizing and word processing.

I would be sorely remiss if I did not speak about the thousands of students whose lives I have been privileged to touch professionally during my five decades in education and in turn who have touched my heart.

The Authors

Irene Eizen

Throughout her educational career spanning over fifty years, Irene has been a leader in mathematics education in elementary, middle, high school, and higher education. Irene received her B.S. and M.Ed. degrees from Temple University, her M.A. in Secondary Mathematics from Arcadia University, and her Ed.D. from Temple University.

Irene began her career teaching elementary and middle school mathematics in the School District of Philadelphia, where she served for twenty years. She became a supervisor of mathematics for the School District of

Philadelphia before pursuing full-time doctoral studies at Temple University.

Early in her career, Irene developed an interest in the extensive use of children's literature to provide a context for mathematics lessons. She lectured on this topic nationally. Irene's book about diverse achievers applies these same principles of context to teach lessons about the strength of diversity.

Beginning in 1985 and through the following decades, she served as an adjunct professor at several colleges, including Arcadia University, Cabrini College, St. Joseph's University, Temple University, the University of Pennsylvania, West Chester University, and Widener University. In her career she has also been a mathematics supervisor, mathematics consultant, and a director for a nationally known mathematics program.

From 1997 to her retirement from public school education in 2007, Irene was the K–12 Supervisor of Mathematics in the Lower Merion School District of Ardmore, Pennsylvania.

In addition to her teaching and supervisory work, Irene founded Do Math for The Fun of It, Inc., a mathematics education consulting firm specializing in professional development at all levels of mathematics education. She also founded the Foundation to Achieve Mathematics Excellence, a tax-qualified educational organization to provide training and support for teachers who wish to increase their content knowledge and enhance their professional development. Through her volunteer efforts toward this end, with help from other nationally recognized mathematics educators, she conducted expansive programs in numerous public, private, and religious schools.

Irene has conducted hundreds of seminars and workshops in all aspects of mathematics education for schools, school districts, and professional organizations at local, state, and national levels. She has been a presenter at annual and regional meetings of teachers and an active member of many national and regional professional organizations. Irene served as Trustee of the Mathematics Education Trust of the National Council of Teachers of Mathematics from 2002 to 2006.

After retiring as a school district administrator, Irene devoted time and energy to giving back to the teaching profession on the faculty of the College of Education and Human Development of her alma mater, Temple University, where she taught until 2020.

Gary Plummer

Gary has been an educator for over forty years and has taught every level from pre-school to graduate school. After graduating from the University of Pittsburgh with a B.S. in early childhood education, he started and directed a pre-school center for his church that served the needs its West Philadelphia community for thirty-nine years. He went on to earn a certification in secondary mathematics from Temple University and an M.Ed. in secondary mathematics from Arcadia University.

In 1988 Gary became a middle school mathematics teacher for the School District of Philadelphia. During his time working in Philadelphia, Gary served as a mathematics specialist, site director for the QUASAR Project, site director for Project FIRST, staff developer for family math, and as an urban systemic initiative professional development leader. He was also an adjunct professor of mathematics education at Arcadia University, the University of Pennsylvania, and Widener University. Gary was also the 1992 Teacher of Excellence Award winner for the Southwest Region in

Philadelphia and one of the Pennsylvania winners for the NSF Presidential Award for Excellence in Mathematics Teaching.

Gary has conducted many seminars and workshops over his career. He has been a speaker at many NCTM National and Regional Conferences as well as local teacher conferences. He was a member of the NAEP Expert Panel on Mathematics Achievement Levels and a coauthor for the book *Investigating Mathematics with PentaBlocks*. Gary spent the last eighteen years of his career doing one of the best jobs he ever had: teaching high school students in Lower Merion School District. In 2017 he retired to do the best job he has ever had: reading books to his great-grandchild.

For more information see
www.diverseachievers.org